The North Georgia Mountains Pocket Companion

– 99 Great North Georgia Destinations –

Second Edition

Brian A. Boyd

Fern Creek Press

North Georgia Mountains Pocket Companion
Second Edition
99 Great North Georgia Destinations

ISBN 978-1-893651-17-3
Fern Creek Press
215 Black Hawk Lane
Clarkesville, Georgia 30523
706.982.3635

Printed in the U.S.A. by Gap Graphics & Printing
Clayton, Georgia, U.S.A.

first printing 2012
second printing 2014

Disclaimer

The author and publisher of this guidebook disclaims any liability or responsibility for any loss of property, accident, injury or death, either directly or indirectly sustained while visiting any of the locations described in this guidebook. Always use caution and good sense—especially when visiting the great outdoors. The publisher has made every reasonable attempt to publish accurate information.

Introduction

Are you ready for some fun and adventure?

The lofty mountains of North Georgia have enticed generations of visitors with their marvelous combination of enchanting beauty and ancient, spellbinding charm. This spectacular region is a marvelous marriage of fascinating history and southern mountain splendor. Quaint mountain towns with names such as Dahlonega, Sautee, Hiawassee, Chickamauga and Toccoa reflect the rich Cherokee history of the region, while other villages such as Clayton, Clarkesville, Blairsville and Ellijay (to name just a few) attest to settlements founded in the pioneer era of the early 1800s. Many of these towns serve as gateways to the relatively narrow swath of peaks and ridges which guard the state's northern boundary, yet each town is delightfully unique and possesses its own enchanting character and charm.

For many, these quaint towns and villages are the main destinations, yet hundreds of thousands of these visitors are drawn each year to the magnificent scenery and spectacular wilderness destinations of North Georgia. Spectacular waterfalls, lofty mountain peaks, scenic trails, spellbinding overlooks, historic and scenic state parks, and the list goes on and on.

So you're ready to go, but perhaps you're a novice to the area, or maybe you just don't know how or where to begin tackling a region so vast. There's a lot to see and do here, and hopefully that's where this little book comes in. From the scores of great destinations found across this region I've tried to whittle it down to just about 100 ideas that provide just a taste of this wonderful region. And without overwhelming the reader with details, I've tried to provide just enough information to educate the reader on each destination, where it is located, and what you can reasonably expect to find and experience when you visit.

Hopefully you can have *more fun* with *less hassle*. So stuff this guide into your purse, pocket or backpack and head to the beautiful North Georgia mountains. Wherever you happen to be, you're probably just around the corner from a classic North Georgia mountains destination.

Before You Go

A word to the wise concerning...

Personal Safety

North Georgia is undoubtedly becoming more "civilized" as thousands of transplants pour into this highly desirable region. Nevertheless, the area contains vast expanses of uncivilized wilderness replete with natural hazards. Numerous deaths and scores of injuries occur each year because of poor preparedness, neglect, and downright stupid behavior by visitors.

A word about waterfall safety: Without doubt the most dangerous attractions in the North Georgia mountains are the magnificent collection of splendid waterfalls. They are beautiful - they are popular - and they can be deadly. Each year people are seriously injured or killed visiting these scenic wonders. Following just a few simple rules could absolutely save a life, maybe yours. These rules seem pretty obvious but tragedies occur when these guidelines are ignored:

- Do not attempt to climb a waterfall; enjoy them from the relative safety of the base or observation deck.
- Stay back from the brink of a waterfall; the rocks are often treacherously slippery! Don't wade or swim upstream from the brink of a waterfall!

General safety: Please obey all posted rules and regulations when in the Chattahoochee National Forest, Georgia state parks, recreation areas or wilderness areas. If possible, DO NOT hike alone and always let someone else know where you are going and when you expect to return. If possible carry a first-aid kit and absolutely *know how to use it.*

Be aware of changing weather conditions, especially the possibility of lightning during the summer thunderstorm season. Hypothermia is a concern in the cold winter months especially if a person becomes wet for an extended period of time. Become familiar with the symptoms of hypothermia and be prepared to act.

Lastly, always lock your automobile and store valuables in the trunk or out of site. Autos parked at isolated trailheads make enticing targets for thieves. Do your part to keep break-ins from happening.

Trail Hazards

It's great to think that every hike into the forest will turn out fine, but there are a few items worth mentioning to keep you on your toes. By all means enjoy your hike and the great scenery, but always be aware of your surroundings. For many hikers poison ivy is enemy #1 in the great outdoors. From April through November you run a good chance of brushing up against this irritating (literally) vine. If you will familiarize yourself with its trademark grouping of three leaves you can probably avoid the resulting miserable experience.

Many varieties of snakes make their homes in the woods and streams of the Blue Ridge. While your chances of seeing a poisonous variety are relatively slim, at least two types are found throughout the region. Copperheads and timber rattlesnakes can be found in just about any North Georgia forest or field. Be on guard, particularly if you are venturing through heavy brush or stepping over an obstacle such as a downed tree. In the span of two weeks in the summer of 2009 I came across an adult copperhead (North Rim Trail - Tallulah Gorge State Park) and a *very impressive* (i.e. terrifying) adult timber rattler (Cohutta Wilderness - Beech Bottom Trail), both parked right in the middle of the trail. Usually if you back off and make a commotion they will gladly yield the trail to you.

Wasps and yellow jackets are another common hazard in the great outdoors. Yellow jackets love to nest in the ground, particularly in rotting stumps or roots. Be aware of where you step at all times. Hornets and wasps often make enormous grey-paper nests that hang from the limbs of trees, and they're not always visible.

In the summer of 2009 while climbing down to the plunge pool at the waterfall on Little Rock Creek near Suches, I grabbed a rhododendron limb for balance and was immediately swarmed by hundreds of white-faced hornets who had made a well-camouflaged nest in the lower limbs. In the eternity of the minute or so that followed I was stung approximately 40 times from head to ankles. In the furious scramble to make my escape I fell several times tearing a rotator cuff and severely spraining an ankle. The hornets finally gave up as I thrashed about in the waterfall's shallow plunge pool. Luckily I was able to hike nearly a mile back to my vehicle. I now carry an epi-pen just in case I have an allergic reaction to a bee sting. Though not always possible try to hike with someone when you can, and *always let someone know where you are*. Your greatest hazard may well be the other humans in the woods at any given time, but use caution and good common sense when in the wild.

99 Destinations?

Even though the book states, "99 great destinations" there's really a lot more in this little book than this number indicates. Take the state parks for instance. Most of them are counted as one destination yet visitors often spend days trying to do everything available to them - hiking, camping, swimming, boating, biking and more.

Be aware that some of these destinations such as state parks and U.S. Forest Service facilities often require a user fee. This can apply to campgrounds, day use areas, biking trails, etc. Georgia state parks require a daily user fee but "frequent flyers" can buy a park pass good for one year of unlimited use. In some cases discounts apply for retirees, veterans, etc. Just don't leave your wallet at home, be prepared!

One last thing, - this guide is obviously the opinionated work of one person. Please don't feel offended if your favorite destination, such as a waterfall, for instance, isn't on the list. Some of the "lesser" falls have been included under other headings. For example, Angel and Panther Falls, while beautiful, are tiny and not too impressive when the creeks are low. They are mentioned as a side note under the Rabun Beach Recreation Area section, however. I am always open to suggestions. If you find something in error please let me know so I can correct it.

Symbols

You'll find these symbols used throughout the guide. In case they're not self-explanatory and you're totally and completely confused by what they mean (I drew them myself and my talents are obviously limited) you can use the cheat sheet here to decipher them.

Table of Contents

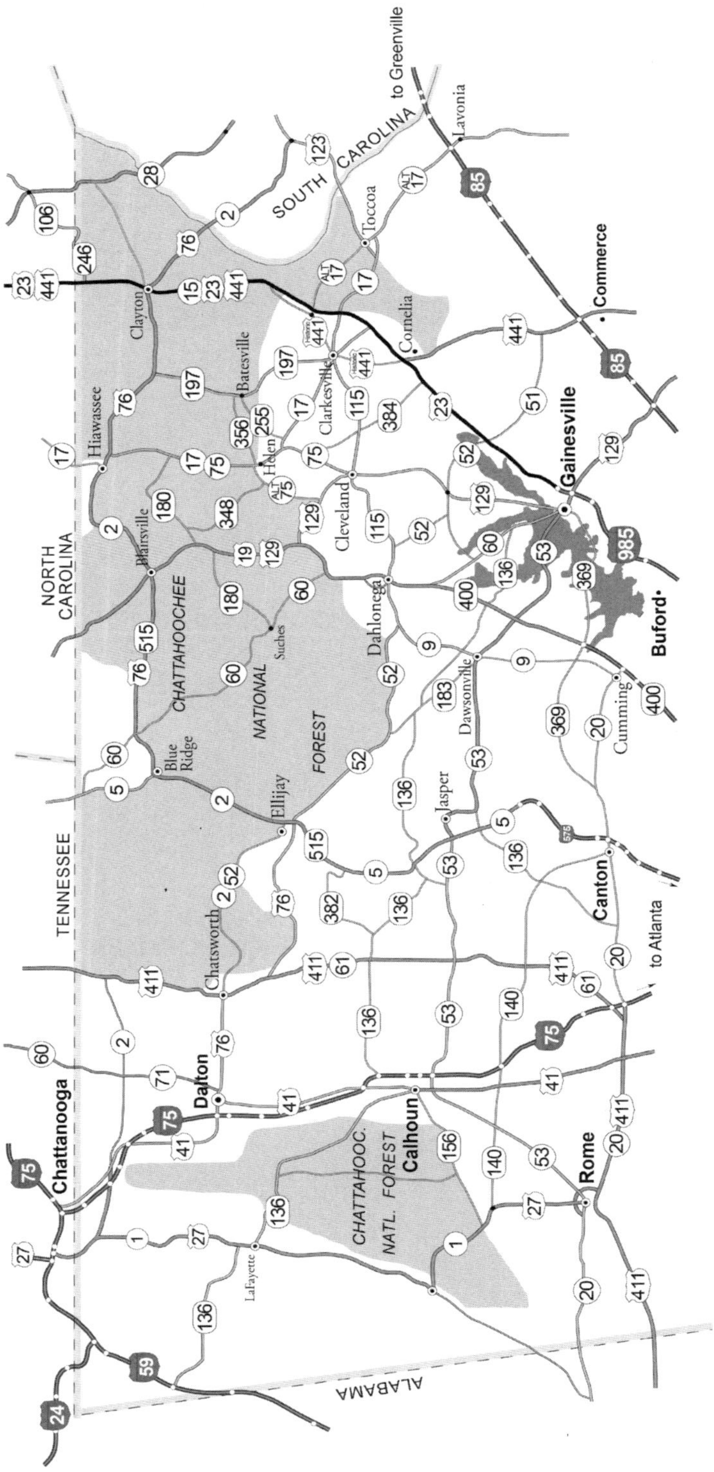

Principal Highways and Towns of North Georgia

1

TOUCHING THE PAST

Dahlonega Gold Museum #1

Commemorating America's First gold rush

Dahlonega Gold Museum State Historic Site
#1 Public Square
Dahlonega, GA 30533
www.gastateparks.org/DahlonegaGoldMuseum
706.864.2257 • Admission fee required
Open 9 am to 5 pm • Sunday 10 am to 5 pm
GPS coordinates:
34.5325°N / 83.9848°W

Between the years 1838 and 1861 more than $6 million worth of gold was coined by the U.S. Mint in the mountain boom town of Dahlonega. The beautiful old Lumpkin County Courthouse, nestled smack dab in the middle of bustling downtown Dahlonega, has been meticulously restored and is now home to the Dahlonega Gold Museum which is dedicated to sharing the dramatic story of one of America's first gold booms. Sample nuggets mined and coins minted in Dahlonega are on display as are photos and relics from this rugged era. A short film demonstrates proper mining technique and provides a fascinating glimpse into the lives of North Georgia's early gold seekers. Come by and see if you don't catch a slight case of *gold fever.*

Directions: You can't miss it. Proceed to downtown Dahlonega - the museum is in the middle of the town square.

#2 Stovall Mill Bridge

Covered bridges - a vanishing historical treasure

Stovall Mill Covered Bridge - White County
Sautee-Nacoochee Valley near Sautee
GPS coordinates:
34.71184°N / 83.65777°W

- **picnic table**
- **foot traffic only**

Once plentiful across the state, Georgia's covered bridges are disappearing as time and the elements take a toll on these historic structures. Beautiful Sautee-Nacoochee Valley is home to one of these gems - the Stovall Mill bridge. Said to be the smallest covered bridge in Georgia (just under 37 feet), this bridge was built in 1895 by Will Purdue. This quaint structure was pictured in the 1951 film *"I'd Climb the Highest Mountain"* starring Susan Heyward and William Lundigan. Some say the bridge is haunted and if you dare venture onto the bridge at night you can supposedly hear the sounds of horse-drawn carriages from the late 19th century. The structure is under the control of the White County Historical Society.

Directions: From Helen proceed south on GA 17/75. Turn left onto GA 17 South towards Clarkesville (note Nacoochee Indian Mound on the left). Drive several miles to the GA 255 intersection in Sautee. Turn left and drive 2.7 miles to the bridge on the right.

Note: Unfortunately graffiti has taken its toll on this rare historic treasure. Hopefully the situation can be remedied in the near future.

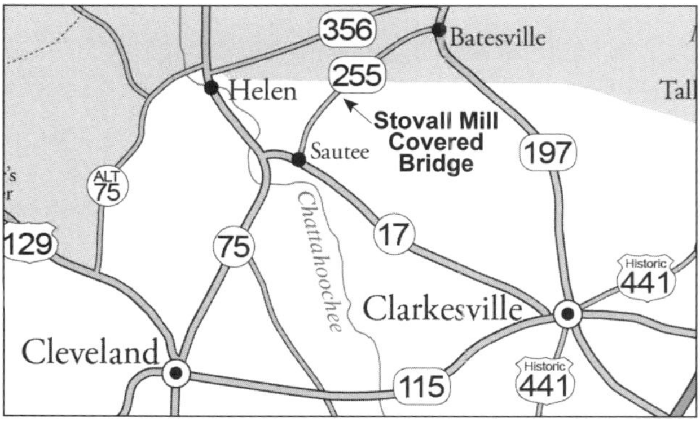

White County Courthouse #3

Historic center of bustling White County

Located in the center of downtown Cleveland
White County Historical Society
P.O. Box 1139 • Cleveland, GA 30528
706.865.5225
Open Thursday, Friday and Saturday 10 am - 3 pm
GPS coordinates:
34.859688°N / 83.763225°W

- **Historic exhibits**
- **convenient to downtown shopping and White County Chamber of Commerce**

According to local historians, slaves from the 19th century molded and fired the thousands of bricks used to construct the historic White County Courthouse, strategically situated in the center of downtown Cleveland. Built just prior to the War Between the States in 1859-1860 the courthouse has been lovingly restored and is now operated by the White County Historical Society. Simplistic yet elegant, the courthouse beckons visitors to explore this historic symbol of early local government. It makes a great starting point for a tour of the former center of this historically significant county.

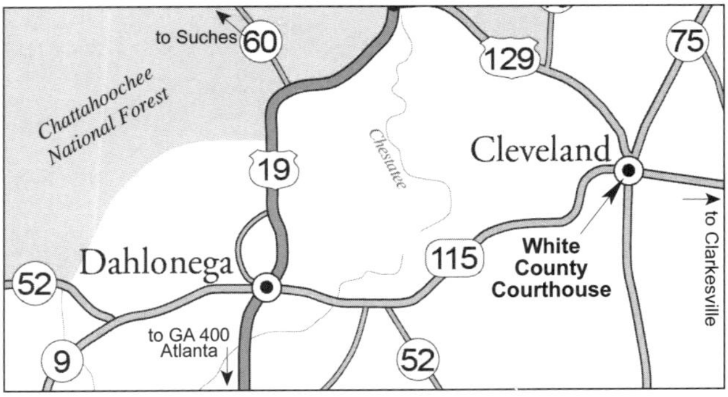

Directions: Located in the center of downtown Cleveland at the junction of GA 115 and U.S. 129.

#4 Track Rock Gap Petroglyphs

Mysterious soapstone carvings produced by Native Americans

Blue Ridge Ranger District
Chattahoochee National Forest
706.745.6928
GPS coordinates:
34.88296°N / 83.8773°W

- **Ancient rock carvings**
- **short hiking loop**

Visitors who are fascinated by the native American history of the region will find the 52-acre Track Rock Archeological Area of particular interest. Several soapstone boulders in this protected area feature ancient carvings known as *petroglyphs*. These petroglyphs resemble circles, crosses, bird tracks, animal tracks and even human footprints.

The Cherokee referred to the Track Rock Gap area as *degayelunha* or "printed place." Meandering footpaths lead past boulders that are somewhat protected by metal cages. Regrettably some have been vandalized in the past by shortsighted individuals. The Track Rock Archeological Area provides a peaceful and unhurried view back into a mysterious era when the mighty Cherokee race ruled the mountains of North Georgia.

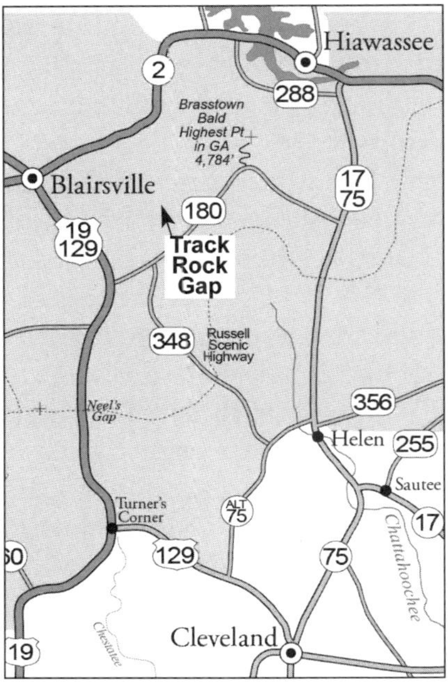

Directions: From the junction of U.S. 19/129 and GA 180 follow GA 180 east to Town Creek Road on the left (1.5 miles beyond GA 348). Proceed 2.2 miles and turn right onto Trackrock Church Road. Proceed 3.1 miles to the stop sign. Turn right onto Trackrock Road and proceed 0.8 mile to the marker on the left.

Alternate route: take U.S. 76 east from Blairsville for 6 miles. Turn right onto Track Rock Road and drive 2.3 miles.

Nacoochee Valley #5

Beautiful mountain valley steeped in history

- **Scenic drive**
- **Historical markers and structures**
- **Interesting inns and shops**

The Nacoochee Indian mound is a prominent landmark alongside busy GA 75 at the valley's western end.

The construction of early roads was a key component in the settlement and ultimate development of North Georgia. The first wagon road through the area was the Unicoi Turnpike, constructed between 1815 and 1817. This rugged "highway" wound through beautiful Nachoochee Valley and the heart of the Cherokee Nation which had thrived here relatively undisturbed for thousands of years. After the development of the turnpike settlers journeyed to the area and began to build homes and farms in the fertile valley. Life was somewhat peaceful until 1838 when the discovery of gold in the area brought miners and industry, followed in the early 20th century by timber companies that logged thousands of acres of virgin forest.

Today motorists wisk through the beautiful valley along modern roads dotted with quaint farms and residences, but much of the valley's rich history is still on display, especially along the three miles that stretch from the GA 75 / GA 17 junction past the intersection with GA 255. A number of historic structures are of special interest and several historical markers provide details of the area's interesting history.

The **Nacoochee Indian Mound** is the first prominent feature. The mound is easily visible along the highway at the 75/17 intersection. According to the historical marker this structure was the center of the ancient Cherokee village *Gauxule* and was reportedly visited by none other than Spanish explorer Hernando Desoto in 1540. More recent research contradicts this claim however. A 1915 excavation discovered 75 native American remains at the site. The mound is deceptively large stretching 190' long, 150' wide and approximately 20' high. The property was part of the Hardman farm at one time and the owners constructed the elaborate gazebo which adorns the top of the mound.

Directly across the highway is **West End**, a beautiful Italiante mansion built by Col. John "Captain" Nichols after the Civil War. In 1903 Dr. Lamartine Hardman bought the property and it remained in his family until purchased for restoration. The Georgia Trust, along with The Trust for Public Land (TPL), Georgia Power Company and the Georgia Department of Natural Resources (DNR), have been working together since 2004 to restore the 23 buildings on the farm with hopes that it can open as a museum in the future.

Crescent Hill Baptist Church

Continue east on GA 17 past historic structures such as **Crescent Hill Baptist Church**, **Nacoochee United Methodist Church**, and the **old trading post**, to name a few. Several of these buildings feature historic markers that tell of their important role in the valley's history. Proceed to Sautee just ahead for an interesting collection of shops and inns.

Continue east to the bridge over Sautee Creek where a historical marker tells the story of **Joe Brown Pikes**. It seems that an old grist mill located here in the mid 1800s was converted to the manufacture of pikes, which were daggers on long poles. Gov. Joesph E. Brown ordered these pikes manufactured to arm the Home Guard during the Civil War. Just north of the bridge are the remains of the dam on the mill site.

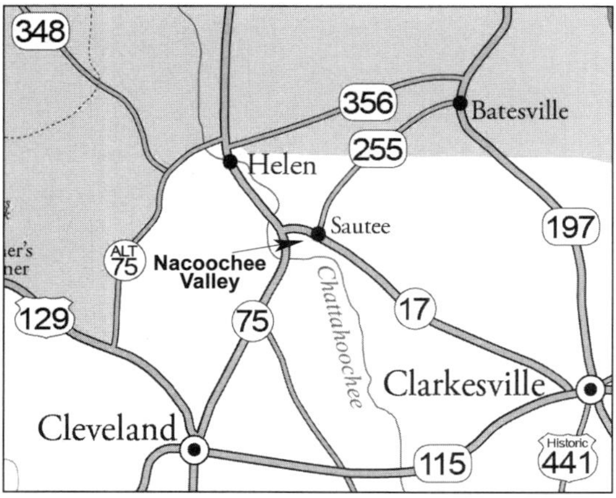

Tallulah Falls Railroad Museum #6

Telling the story of the "Total Failure" Railroad

Highway 441
Rabun Gap, GA 30568
GPS coordinates:
34.95915°N / 83.38655°W

- **Normal hours: Friday, Saturday and Sunday (Spring - Fall)**
- **706.746.7467 Rabun Gap-Nacoochee School number**
- **Nominal admission fee**

The wonderful Tallulah Falls Railroad, known affectionately as the "Total Failure" Railroad, was one of the most interesting and unique shortline railroads ever constructed. The TFRR traveled 58 dramatic miles over 42 wonderful rickety wooden trestles as it ran from Cornelia, Georgia to Franklin, North Carolina.

Constructed primarily between 1898 and 1905, the railroad was abandoned in 1961 due to ongoing financial difficulties. In fact the railroad was profitable for only a few years in over six decades of operation. During its glory years the "Old TF" carried thousands of passengers through this rugged mountain region and effectively "opened up" the region to settlement and development. The line retained a look of yesteryear that attracted Hollywood movie makers. Several scenes from the 1950s classics *"I'd Climb the Highest Mountain"* and much of the action in Disney's *"The Great Locomotive Chase"* was filmed on the Tallulah Falls Railroad.

The TFRR Museum is the result of years of hard work by Dess Oliver, renowned Industrial Arts instructor at Rabun Gap-Nacoochee School (just across the highway from the museum). Dess, along with scores of his former students, lovingly built the museum including the full-size 2-ft. gauge locomotive, passenger car, flat car and caboose on display. The museum also features scores of authentic TFRR relics and photos.

Directions: The Tallulah Falls Railroad Museum is located approximately 7 miles north of Clayton on the right side of U.S. 441, directly across from Rabun Gap-Nacoochee School.

#7 Barker's Creek Mill

These structures were once the centers of their communities

The Hambidge Center for Creative Arts & Sciences
105 Hambidge Court
Rabun Gap, GA 30568
706.746.5718
www.hambidge.org
GPS coordinates:
34.9977°N / 83.4497°W

- **historic working mill**
- **nice spot for picnic**
- **arts center**

Located on the expansive grounds of the renowned Hambidge Center for creative Arts & Sciences near Dillard, this historic structure is a throwback to the days when mills were the commercial centers of isolated rural communities. Barker's Creek Mill was constructed in 1944 for Hambidge Center founder Mary Hambidge. Several other mills have operated along the creek nearly continually over the past 175 years.

The mill is normally open to the public on warm weather weekends, and typically grinds corn meal the first weekend each month. Check with the Hambidge Center office for exact times of operation. And while you're here be sure to visit the historic Hambidge Center just back down the road. The 600-acre center was one of the first artist communities in the United States and today offers a number of extraordinary programs for artists on its beautiful campus which features several fascinating structures, beautifully landscaped grounds and walking paths.

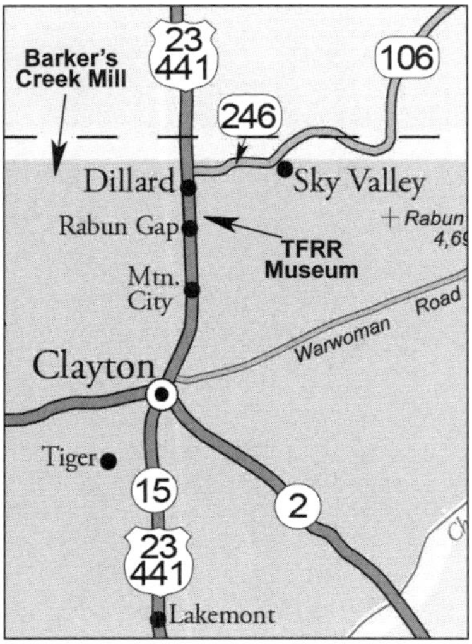

Directions: From U.S. 441 in Dillard turn west onto Betty's Creek Road and proceed approximately 4 miles to the Hambidge Center. The mill is an additional one mile down Betty's Creek Road. Look for the sign and pull-off on the left.

Foxfire Museum & Heritage Center #8

Preserving Appalachian history and culture

Foxfire Museum
200 Foxfire Lane
Mountain City, GA 30562
706.746-5828
GPS coordinates:
34.91235°N / 83.39570°W

- **Historic Structures**
- **Guided group tours or self-guided walks**
- **Gift Shop**
- **Walking trails**
- **Open 8:30am–4:30pm Mon-Sat**
- **Admission fee**

The Museum's Chapel

The world-renowned Foxfire program originated right here in Rabun County in 1966 with *Foxfire Magazine,* a creative attempt to motivate local high school English students toward greater learning. Today, over 45 years and 9 million books later Foxfire continues as a leader in the successful learner-centered, community-based educational approach.

The Foxfire Museum, situated on the forested slopes of rugged Black Rock Mountain, hosts an impressive collection of over 20 log structures including a chapel, gristmill, smokehouse and a fascinating display of Appalachian tools and equipment, all right at home in a small community setting. After your self-guided walking tour be sure to visit the gift shop and browse the wonderful collection of regional pottery, soaps, books and more (including the *Foxfire* series, of course).

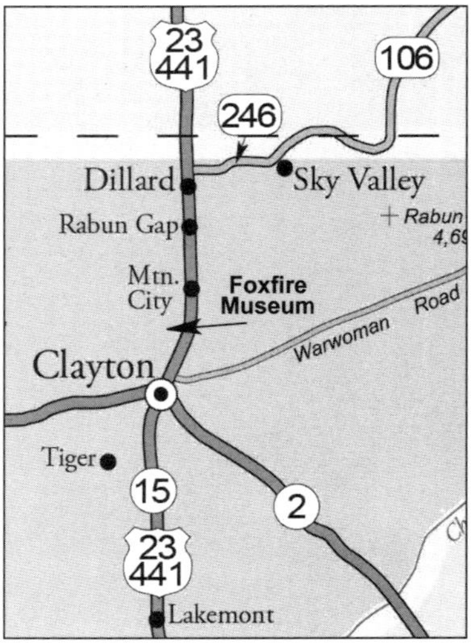

Directions: From U.S. 441 in Mountain City turn west onto Black Rock Mountain Parkway and follow the signs to the Museum driveway. Park at the gift shop.

#9 Traveler's Rest

Originally a 19th century bed and breakfast

Traveler's Rest Historic Site
4339 Riverdale Road
Toccoa, GA 30577
706.886.2256
call for hours
GPS coordinates:
34.6091°N / 83.243°W

- **National Historic Landmark**
- **Camping nearby at Lake Tugaloo State Park**
- **Admission Fee**

Constructed in 1815 by James Wyly as an inn for stagecoach passengers, Traveler's Rest later served as the plantation home of Devereaux Jarrett. Jarrett, one of the area's most prosperous citizens, bought the site in 1833 and made it the centerpiece of his bustling 14,000+ acre plantation not far from the Tugaloo River, one of the Savannah River's headwater streams. The inn was strategically located along two frequently traveled early roads of the day: the Federal Road, which ran from New England south to Florida; and the Unicoi Turnpike, which carried early travelers from northeastern Georgia into Tennessee.

Three generations of Jarretts inhabited the home until 1955 when the State of Georgia purchased the house and remaining acreage for $8,000. Traveler's Rest was designated a National Historic Landmark in 1964.

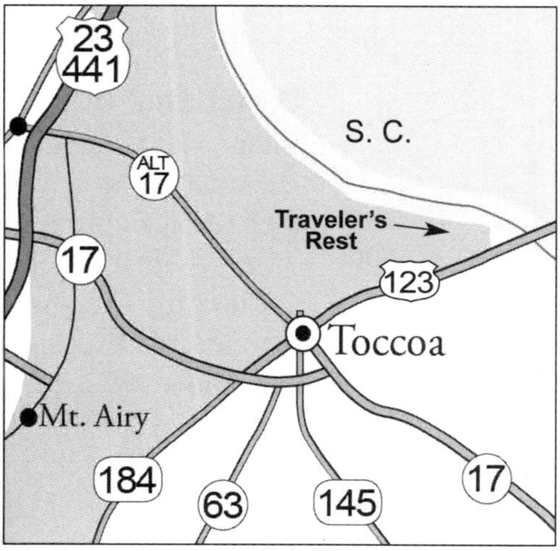

Directions: Travelers Rest is located 6 miles east of Toccoa. Take U.S. 123 east from Toccoa. Turn left onto Riverdale Road (look for the Traveler's Rest sign) and drive approximately 0.3 mile.

Chief Vann House #10

Historic plantation of successful Cherokee leader

82 Georgia Hwy 225
Chatsworth, GA 30705
www.gastateparks.org
706.695.2598
Open Thurs, Fri and Sat
GPS coordinates:
34.76349°N / 83.8212°W

- **Historic exhibits**
- **Guided house tours**
- **Nature trail**
- **Picnic area**
- **Admission fee**

This 109-acre historic site in Murray County near Chatsworth was once the site of a bustling plantation owned by Cherokee businessman James Vann. Some have even referred to it as *the* showplace of the Cherokee nation. At its peak Vann's plantation covered over 1,000 acres and was the most prosperous farm of its type in the Cherokee region. The beautiful 2-1/2 story brick home built by Vann in 1804 remains as the centerpiece of the well-preserved collection of structures.

Vann was tragically murdered in 1809 and the plantation came under the control of his son, Joseph. Most of Vann's Cherokee descendants were relocated west in the infamous and tragic "Trail of Tears" in the 1830s.

Guided tours of the wonderfully preserved home are offered and well worthwhile. The house has an interesting assortment of antiques and carefully crafted hand carvings. Of special architectural interest is the cantilevered "floating staircase."

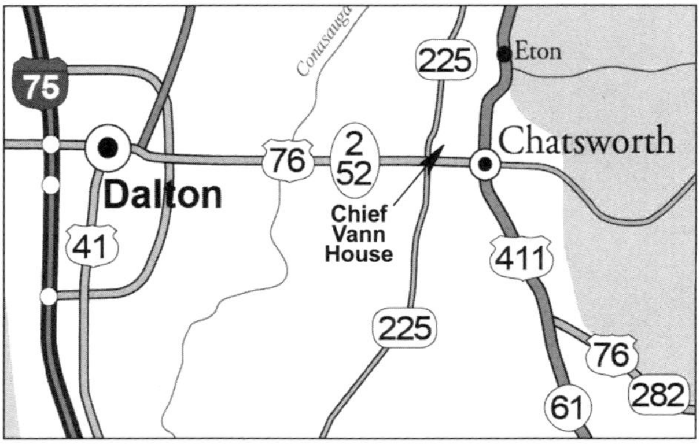

Directions: Chief Vann House State Historic Site is located about two miles west of Chatsworth at the GA 52/GA 225 intersection.

#11 New Echota Historic Site

The official starting point for the "Trail of Tears"

1211 Chatsworth Hwy NE
Calhoun, GA 30701
706.624.1301
Open Thurs, Fri, and Sat
www.gastateparks.org
GPS coordinates:
34.5409°N / 84.909°W

- **Historic exhibits & research library**
- **Nature trail**
- **Fishing/boat ramp**
- **Admission fee**

In 1825 the Cherokee legislature established their new capital along the Oostanaula River near modern-day Calhoun. The site carries great significance in Cherokee history as it is where the infamous "Trail of Tears," the forced relocation of the Cherokee from Georgia began. It is significant for a number of accomplishments such as the first native American newspaper which was published here. New Echota is the earliest known attempt in national self government by a native American tribe. It was also the site of a treaty signing which gave up Cherokee claims to all lands east of the Mississippi River.

Visitors to site today are able to see 12 original and reconstructed buildings; among these are the court house, council house, print shop, an early 1800s store and other agricultural buildings such as a smoke house, corn crib and barns. A short one-mile nature trail leads to other sites. The visitor center features an interesting selection of historical exhibits and a short educational film.

Directions: New Echota is located one mile east of I-75 (exit 317) on GA 225 in Calhoun.

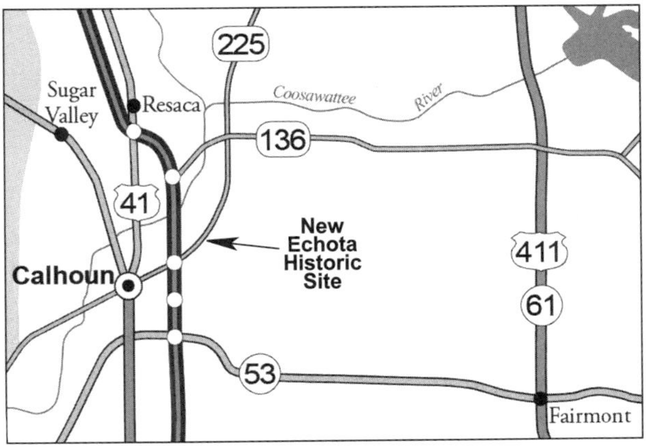

Chickamauga Battlefield #12

Part of the Chickamauga & Chattanooga National Military Park

3370 LaFayette Road
Fort Ogelthorpe, GA 30742
706.866.9241
www.nps.gov/chch/index.htm
GPS coordinates:
34.9403°N / 85.2599°W

- **Historic exhibits**
- **Driving tour**
- **Hiking trails**

Dedicated in 1895, Chickamauga Battlefield Park entails 5,300 acres that was the location of the last major Confederate victory in the Civil War. The Union and Confederate armies met here in September, 1863 as part of the larger battle for Chattanooga. A 7-mile auto tour of the battlefield is detailed in the park brochure. There are exhibits, historical markers, monuments and several dozen miles of trails. A "dial and discover" cell phone tour has also been created to enhance your tour.

The visitor center is a great place to start and orient oneself for the visit. The short orientation film is quite valuable. The center features a number of educational exhibits as well as a fiber-optic battlefield map and the Claud E. and Zenada O. Fuller Collection of American Military Shoulder Arms. If you enjoy the Chickamauga battlefield experience be sure to make the short drive to Chattanooga and visit the Lookout Mountain Battlefield and Moccasin Bend National Archeological District. The park gained inclusion to the National Register of Historic Places in 1966. Be sure to check out www.nps.gov/chch/index.htm for a complete rundown on the park.

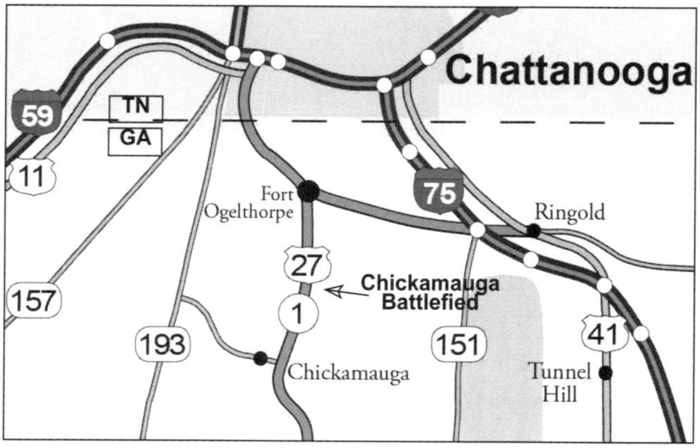

Directions: The park is located approximately 7 miles south of Fort Ogelthorpe on U.S. 27/GA 1.

2

North Georgia's STATE PARKS

Tallulah Lake - Tallulah Gorge State Park

Unicoi State Park #13

One of Georgia's most popular state parks

Unicoi State Park - White County
1788 GA 356 • Helen 30545
706.878.3982
located 3 miles northeast of Helen
www.gastateparks.org
GPS Coordinates:
34.7238°N / 83.7254°W

- **Boating**
- **Fishing**
- **Swimming**
- **Hiking**
- **Camping, cabins, lodge and conference center**
- **Picnicking**
- **Biking**

Beautiful Unicoi State Park encompasses over 1,000 pristine acres just five minutes from bustling alpine Helen. Tens of thousands of visitors come to the park each year and enjoy a wide range of outdoor activities and an equally wide range of accommodations which ranges from roughing it in a tent to relaxing in style in the beautiful Unicoi lodge.

Accommodations: Unicoi features five camping areas with 84 tent, trailer and RV sites. If you'd like your visit a bit more civilized try the 100-room lodge with restaurant. Call 1.800.864.7275 for reservations.

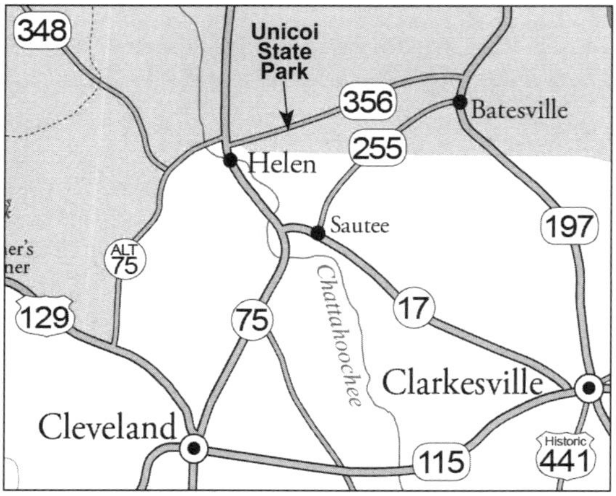

Unicoi Lake: Beautiful 53-acre Unicoi Lake features a pretty sandy beach along its northern end with an unsupervised swimming area. Canoe and paddle boat rentals are available in-season. The 2.4-mile Unicoi Lake Trail features several great observation decks offering big views of the lake.

Fishing: Trout fishing is quite popular in the park, both in Unicoi Lake and on Smith Creek, the lake's major tributary stream. Portions of the lake banks are relatively clear of underbrush and several large decks scattered around the lake offers a good fishing platform for novices. All Georgia fishing rules and regulations apply.

Hiking: Unicoi features several excellent hiking trails. The 2.4-mile **Unicoi Lake Trail** is perhaps the most popular, but hikers may also choose the 0.3-mile **Frog Pond Nature Trail**, 2-mile **Bottoms Loop Trail** or the 3-mile **Unicoi/ Helen Trail**. The most challenging park path is the 5-mile **Smith Creek Trail** (which ironically doesn't see much of Smith Creek until it nears its end at magnificent Anna Ruby Falls). Anna Ruby is located north of the park in the USFS Anna Ruby Falls Scenic Area.

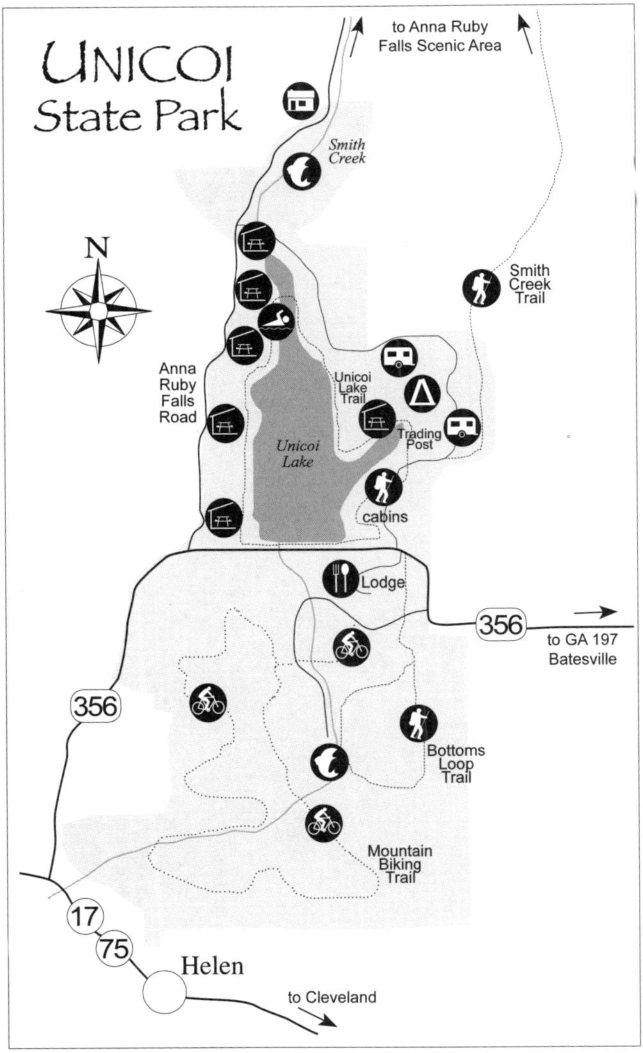

Picnicking: Several picnic areas are scattered around the park including seven covered shelters. Contact the park if you wish to reserve a shelter ($45).

Tennis: Four lighted courts are located near the lodge.

Biking: The park features a 7.5-mile single-track biking trail that is rated moderate to strenuous.

Vogel State Park #14

Georgia's second oldest state park

Vogel State Park - Union County
7485 Vogel State Park Road
Blairsville, GA 30512
706.745.2628 • www.gastateparks.org
GPS Coordinates:
34.73203°N / 83.91713°W

- **Pedal boats**
- **Fishing**
- **Swimming**
- **Hiking**
- **Camping & cabins**
- **Picnicking**
- **Mini golf**

Georgia's second oldest state park was founded back in 1928 when brothers August and Fred Vogel, Jr. donated a remarkably beautiful section of mountain property at the base of rugged Blood Mountain south of Blairsville to the state of Georgia. Today the magnificent 280-acre park is one of Georgia's most popular parks and undeniably one of the most scenic. The Vogel brothers had used bark harvested from oak and hemlock trees on the property to tan leather in their Wisconsin tannery in the early 20th century.

Vogel State Park is situated at a cool 2,500' elevation and is understandably quite popular during the hot summer months. Try to plan your visit in order to avoid the busy warm-weather weekends if possible. Vogel offers a surprisingly wide array of outdoor activities for such

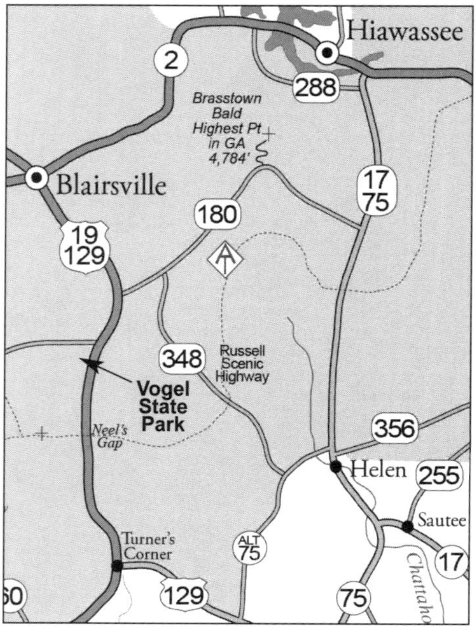

a small park, and dozens of other interesting destinations are a short drive (or hike) away.

Accommodations: Vogel State Park offers 95 tent and trailer campsites complete with electrical hook-ups and water, as well as 15 primitive walk-in sites. A pioneer camping area is also available for larger groups (by reservation only). Thirty-six very popular cottages of varying sizes are also available for rental. For reservations call 800.864.7275.

Lake Trahlyta: Sparkling Wolf Creek tumbles south from rugged Blood Mountain until it is temporarily stilled by the cold, clear waters of Trahlyta Lake. This 22-acre gem is the centerpiece of the park and features a swimming beach and bathhouse. Motorized private boats are not permitted on the lake but a fleet of vintage pedal boats is available for rental. If you have your own canoe, a launch ramp is available.

Fishing: Fishing is extremely popular in the park with trout, bass and bream plentiful. The lake is regularly stocked with trout.

Picnicking: Four picnic shelters and 65 picnic tables make Vogel a favorite destination for this most important culinary activity. Call to reserve a group shelter (fee).

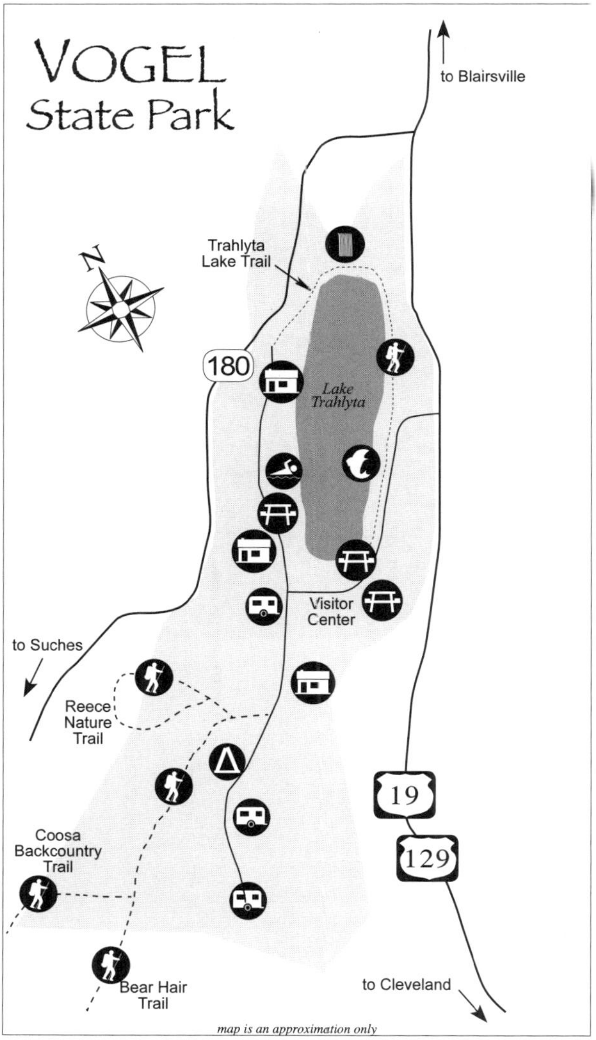

Hiking: Vogel offers several great hiking trails. Two of the hikes falling into the "easy" category include the one-mile **Trahlyta Lake Trail** and the 0.6-mile **Byron Reece Nature Trail**. The lake trail makes a complete circle around the beautiful 22-acre lake and features many excellent views of the park and surrounding mountains. On the south end of the lake, the short **Falls Bottom Trail** drops down to an observation deck overlooking pretty Trahlyta Falls.

Those looking for more of a challenge may wish to tackle the 4-mile **Bear Hair Trail** or the strenuous 12.5-mile **Coosa Backcountry Trail** (permit required) which boasts a challenging 2,000' elevation gain.

Other great footpaths are just a short drive away. The legendary Appalachian Trail crosses U.S. 19/129 just a few miles north of the park at Neels Gap. Several trails, including the A.T., transport hikers to the summit of lofty 4,461' Blood Mountain and back down to neighboring Winfield Scott Recreation Area along GA 180.

Trahlyta Falls at the end of the Falls Bottom Trail

#15 Amicalola Falls State Park

Georgia's gateway to the famed Appalachian Trail

Amicalola Falls State Park - Dawson County
240 Amicalola Falls State Park Road • Dawsonville, GA 30534
706.265.4703 • www.gastateparks.org
GPS Coordinates:
34.56064°N / 84.24797°W

- **One of the highest waterfalls in the eastern U.S.**
- **campground**
- **lodge & cottages**
- **hiking**
- **Appalachian Approach Trail**
- **picnicking**
- **Len Foote Hike Inn**
- **fishing**

A*makalola*, or "tumbling waters" as it was appropriately known to the native Cherokee, is the centerpiece of this 829-acre state park which is prominent both for its majestic 700-foot waterfall and its proximity to the southern terminus of the legendary Appalachian Trail. It's strategic location along the southern end of the Appalachians and short distance to Atlanta make it one of Georgia's most popular parks.

Accommodations: Just a generation ago if you desired to spend a few days in the park you could choose between a rustic cabin or reserve a spot in the park's campground. Today there is a wide range of accommodations ranging from the 57-room lodge near the brink of Amicalola Falls, 24 campsites with water and electrical hookups, or one of 14 fully equipped cottages. Call 800.864.7275 for campground reservations and 800.573.9656 for lodge reservations.

Picnic facilities: With so much beauty to enjoy Amicalola Falls State Park is a great place for a picnic. Find a good spot along the creek or choose from dozens of tables and 5 picnic shelters scattered about the park. You must call ahead in order to reserve a shelter for a large group (fee required).

Len Foote Hike Inn: This accommodation isn't exactly *in* the park, and that's kind of the idea. The Len Foote Hike Inn is perfect for those who'd like to take a long hike but also want to hit a nice, soft mattress at the end of the trail. Hike Inn is reached via an easy to moderate 5-mile hike. Springer Mountain, the southern terminus of the Appalachian Trail, is only 4.5 miles from the inn.

The Inn's mission is to "make experiencing nature easy, and help protect it through education and recreation." The inn offers 20 private guest rooms with hot showers and home-cooked meals. Go to http://hike-inn.com/ for more information.

Fishing: Fishing is permitted in the reflection pool below the falls and in Little Amicalola Creek during trout season.

Hiking: The trail everyone is interested in is the 8.1-mile blue-blazed **Appalachian Trail Approach Trail**. This heavily used pathway winds up the starting point (or ending point depending upon which direction you hike) of the Appalachian Trail atop Springer Mountain. The approach trail is rated moderate to strenuous and isn't really a good choice for novice hikers - it's both long and hard, not a good combination for the beginner. A portion of this trail runs from the reflection pool at the base of the waterfall up to a wonderful viewing platform.

Other trails include the strenuous one-mile **East Ridge Trail**, the one-mile **Mountain Laurel Loop,** and the moderate 0.6-mile **Creek Trail**. The 0.3-mile **West Ridge Falls Access Trail** is handicapped accessible and provides a nice view of the waterfall.

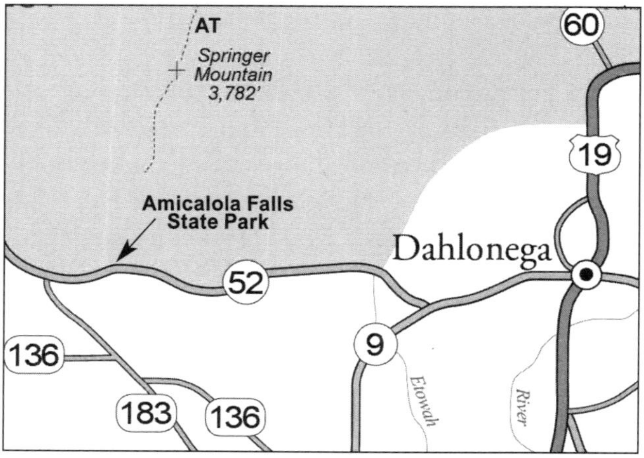

Amicalola
Falls State Park

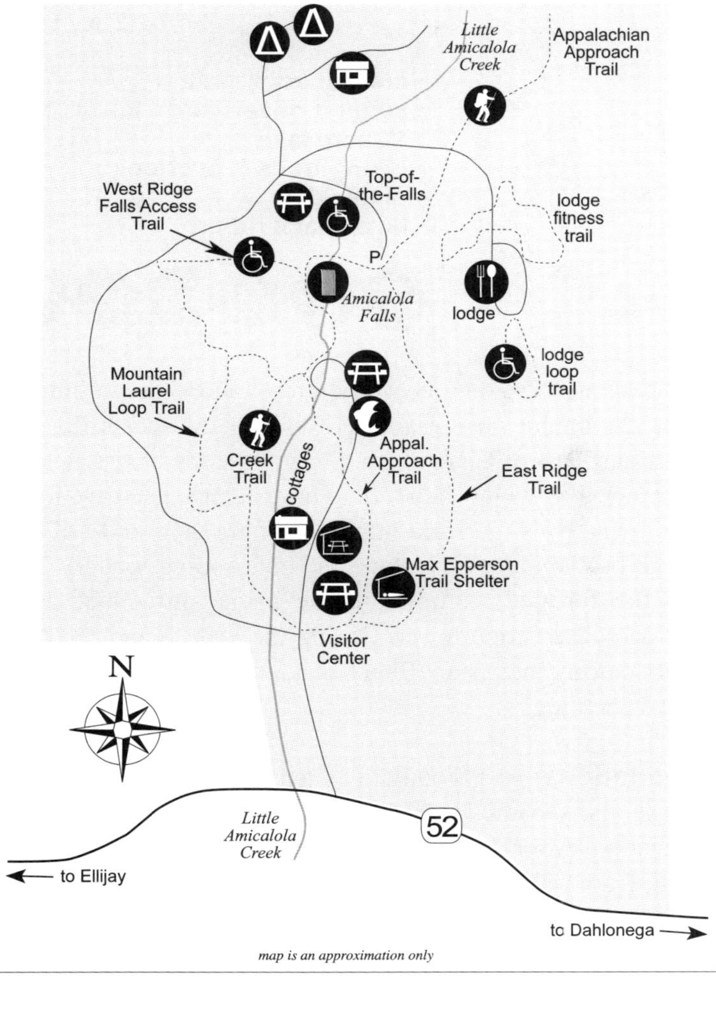

map is an approximation only

Fort Mountain State Park #16

Site of a mysterious stone wall that baffles historians

Fort Mountain State Park - Murray County
181 Fort Mountain State Park Road
Chatsworth, GA 30705
706.422.1932 • www.gastateparks.org
GPS Coordinates:
34.7612°N / 84.6997°W

- **historic rock wall**
- **summit observation tower**
- **17-acre lake**
- **hiking trails & overlooks**
- **picnicking**
- **horseback riding**

A mysterious 855-foot rock wall stretches across the summit of 2,854' Fort Mountain on the northern end of this beautiful 3,712-acre park just east of Chatsworth. Several theories exist as to its exact origin, but the wall is widely believed to have been a defensive fortification constructed by native Americans hundreds, if not thousands, of years ago.

The park brims with rich history and outstanding scenery. The views from atop the forested summit are the prime attraction, particularly from the stone observation tower. During the leafless months of late fall through early spring the distant Blue Ridge peaks to the north and east are particularly appealing.

Accommodations: Fort Mountain State Park features 70 tent and trailer sites, 4 backcountry camps as well as 15 cottages for those seeking a bit more civilization. Several primitive walk-in sites are located along the 8.2-mile Gahuti Trail. Call 800.864.7275 for campground reservations.

Fort Mountain Lake: This "mountain top" park also features 17-acre Fort Mountain Lake. Cold and clear, this scenic lake features a swimming beach, bathhouse, pedal boats and miniature golf during the warm summer season.

Picnicking: There's no shortage of great picnic sites - 7 shelters and over 100 picnic tables are scattered around the lake.

Hiking: There is a wide variety of hiking opportunities at Fort Mountain State Park - 14 miles in fact. The most popular route is the 1.3-mile **Old Fort Trail** which winds up to the summit of Fort Mountain passing the renowned rock wall.

A beautiful 38-foot observation tower rises proudly above the summit, looking something like the type of structure you'd find in Gothic Britain. The tower was constructed by the Civilian Conservation Corps in the 1930s. From the tower stroll west out to the breathtaking Chatsworth Overlook and gaze across the scenic valley region west of Georgia's Blue Ridge mountains.

Other hiking trails include the challenging 8.2-mile **Gahuti Trail** which offers wilderness camping opportunities and a number of outstanding vistas.

For the novice, the 1.2-mile **Lake Loop Trail** is a great way to stretch the legs and take in the placid lake scenery.

Mountain Biking: The park features 4 biking paths of varied degrees of challenge. The 1.2-mile **Lake Loop** is great for beginners but you'll have to share the path with hikers. The moderate **Gold Mine Loop** is 6 miles long; the 7-mile **Cool Springs Loop** is rated difficult with some steep climbs and descents. The ultimate in Fort Mountain biking is the challenging 14.6-mile **East/West Loop** that includes over 1500' of elevation change. A $3 per biker fee is required on all but the lake loop.

Horseback Riding: For something a bit off the trodden path, there are over 37 miles of horse trails nearby with rentals available. Call 706.517.4906 for more information. Email: cmc_farms@yahoo.com.

Fort Mountain Stables
548 Cliff Mine Road
Chatsworth, GA

A Fort Mountain State Park map is on the next page.

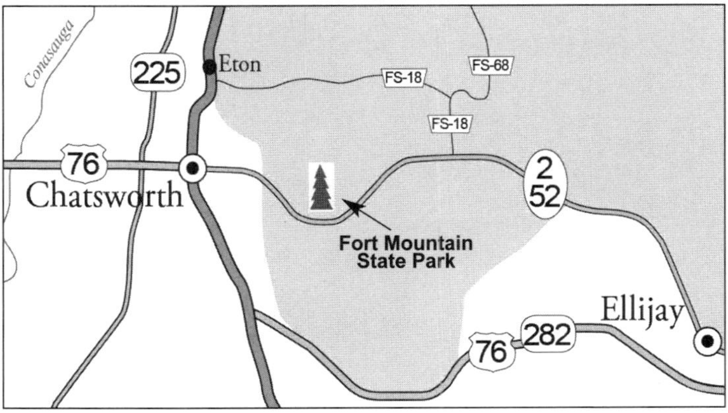

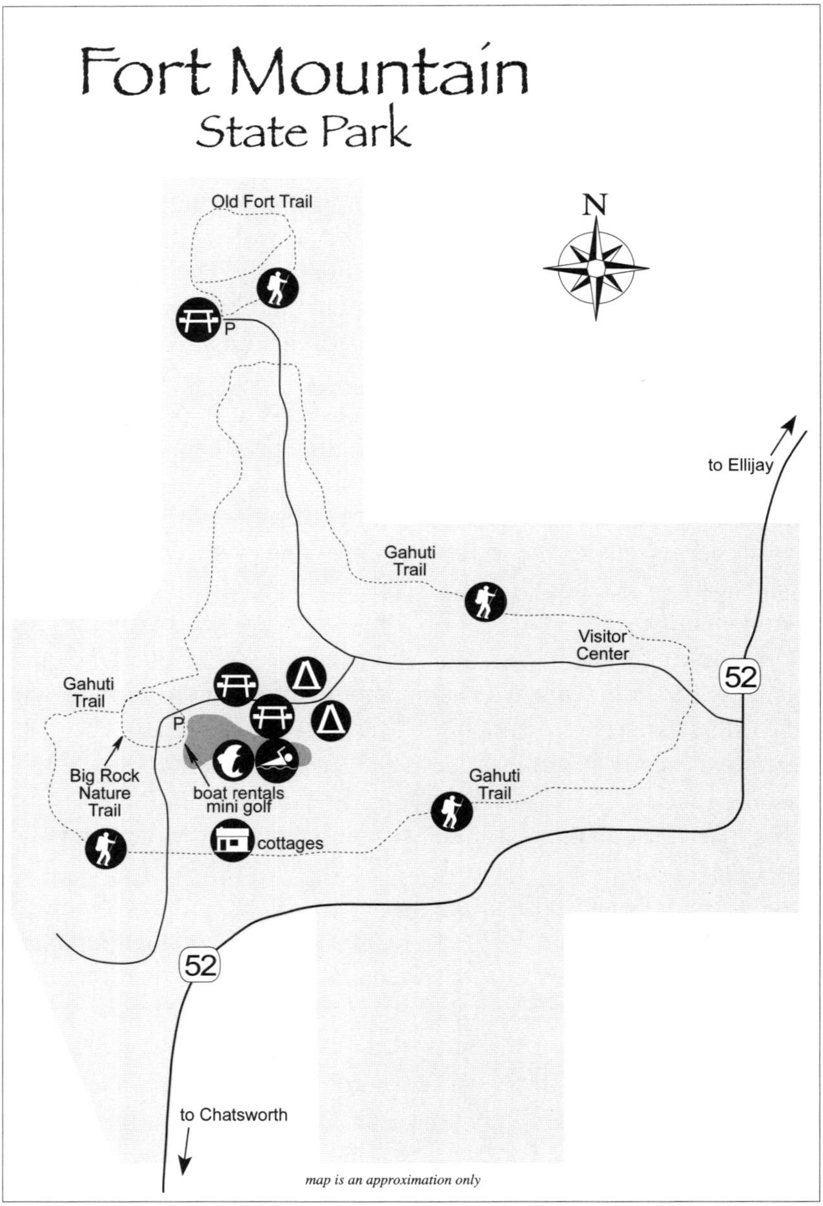
Fort Mountain
State Park
N
Old Fort Trail
P
Gahuti
Trail
to Ellijay
Visitor
Center
52
Gahuti
Trail
P
Big Rock
Nature
Trail
boat rentals
mini golf
Gahuti
Trail
cottages
52
to Chatsworth
map is an approximation only

#17 Black Rock Mountain State Park

Georgia's highest state park offers magnificent vistas

Black Rock Mountain State Park - Rabun County
3085 Black Rock Mountain Parkway
Mountain City, GA 30562
706.746.2141
www.gastateparks.org
GPS Coordinates:
34.91724°N / 083.40373°W

- **six peaks above 3,000' elevation**
- **beautiful vistas**
- **hiking trails**
- **picnic shelters**
- **camping & cottages**
- **fishing lake**
- **closed December 1 through March 15**

Late afternoon at the magnificent Tennessee Rock Overlook. photo by Joseph Boyd

Lofty Black Rock Mountain State Park got its name from the towering sheer cliffs of dark granite located just below the park's main visitor center near the mountain's summit. Among Georgia's many state parks and historic sites, Black Rock is unique in that it is Georgia's highest state park. The park encompasses 1,743 acres and features six peaks exceeding the 3,000' mark. It's also interesting to note that the park straddles the eastern continental divide. Rainfall on the park's southern flanks flows into the Chattooga River/Savannah River basin, eventually emptying into the Atlantic Ocean; precipitation falling on the north side of the mountain takes a tortuous path to the Gulf of Mexico via the Little Tennessee/Tennessee/ Ohio and Mississippi Rivers.

Accommodations: For a "mountain top" park Black Rock Mountain State Park offers a surprisingly large number of accommodations. Guests may choose from 10 rental cottages, 44 tent, trailer and rv campsites, 12 walk-in campsites, 4 back country campsites and a pioneer group campground.

Black Rock Lake: You might not expect a mountain top park to have a lake, but Black Rock Mountain State Park does indeed. It's located on the north end of the park near Wolffork Valley and over a thousand feet below the summit (at an elevation of 2,241'). Seventeen-acre Black Rock Lake offers surprisingly good fishing for bass, bream, catfish and trout. A relatively flat 0.85-mile trail circles the lake.

Picnicking: Two large covered pavilions provide sheltered picnicking for groups or individuals and plenty of other picnic tables are scattered about the area near the visitor center and Black Rock overlook. Adjacent to one of the pavilions is a spacious playground area for the kids.

Hiking Trails: Black Rock Mountain State Park features some great hiking - nearly 11 miles in fact. In my opinion these trails may offer some of the best scenery in the entire Georgia state park system.

From the shortest to the longest, here goes: The shortest is the 0.25 -mile **Ada-hi Falls Trail** which drops down to a trickling cascade high in the Taylor Creek watershed. The only really easy hike in the park is the 0.85-mile **Black Rock Lake Trail** which circles the lake, and is a nice hike for those with small children or looking for a gentle scenic stroll.

The magnificent **Tennessee Rock Trail** is next. This 2.2-mile path offers a few challenges as it traverses the mountain's cool, moist north-facing cove. The high point of the hike (literally and figuratively as well) is the stop at the Tennessee Rock overlook which gazes across beautiful Wolffork Valley and all the way into the Smokies (on exceptionally clear days). Along the summit ridgeline the trail follows the path of the eastern continental divide.

The most challenging of the park's trails is the 7.2-mile **James Edmonds Backcountry Trail**. This is a real heart-pumper with overall elevation changes well over 1,000 vertical feet. Highlights are visits to a stunning overlook atop Lookoff Mountain as well as Black Rock Lake. Rated moderate to strenuous.

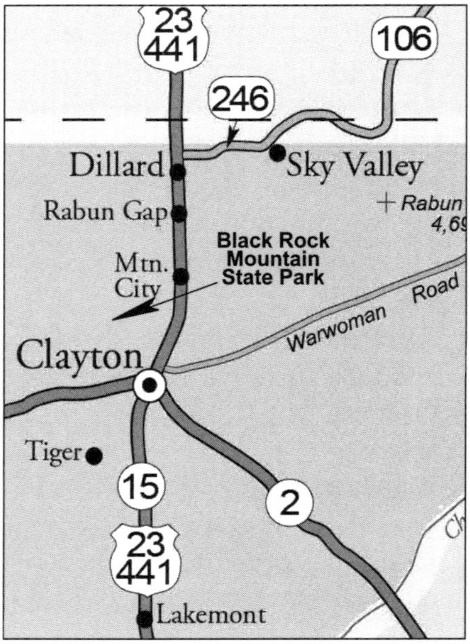

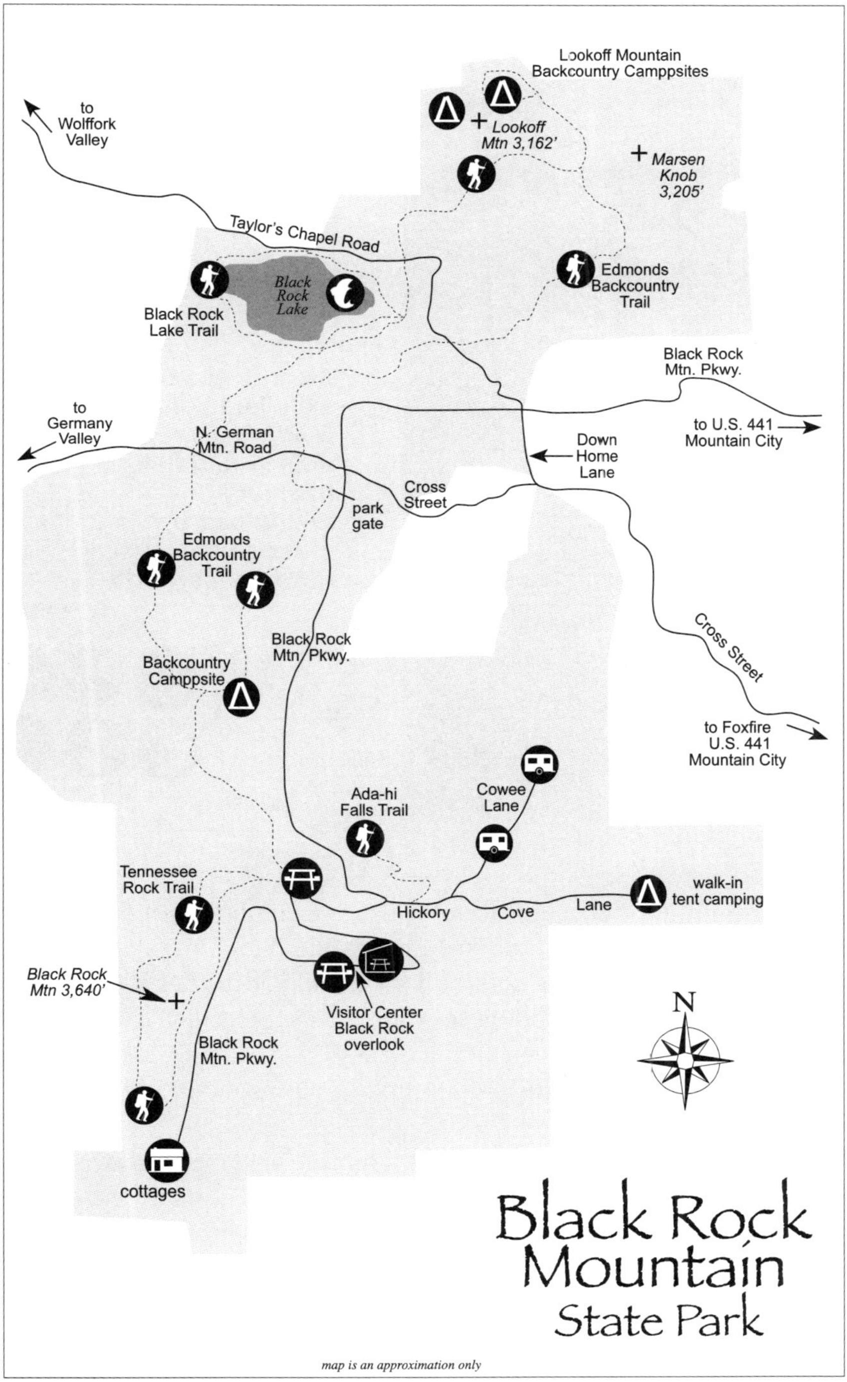
Lookoff Mountain
Backcountry Camppsites
Lookoff
Mtn 3,162'
Marsen
Knob
3,205'
to
Wolffork
Valley
Taylor's Chapel Road
Black
Rock
Lake
Black Rock
Lake Trail
Edmonds
Backcountry
Trail
Black Rock
Mtn. Pkwy.
to U.S. 441
Mountain City
to
Germany
Valley
N. German
Mtn. Road
Down
Home
Lane
Cross
Street
park
gate
Edmonds
Backcountry
Trail
Black Rock
Mtn. Pkwy.
Backcountry
Camppsite
Cross Street
to Foxfire
U.S. 441
Mountain City
Cowee
Lane
Ada-hi
Falls Trail
Tennessee
Rock Trail
Hickory
Cove
Lane
walk-in
tent camping
Black Rock
Mtn 3,640'
Visitor Center
Black Rock
overlook
Black Rock
Mtn. Pkwy.
N
cottages
Black Rock
Mountain
State Park
map is an approximation only

Moccasin Creek State Park #18

Popular park on the western shore of beautiful Lake Burton

Moccasin Creek State Park - Rabun County
3655 GA Hwy 197
Clarkesville, GA 30523
706.947.3194
www.gastateparks.org
GPS Coordinates:
34.84583°N / 083.5875°W

Pretty Hemlock Falls - an easy hike from Moccasin Creek State Park

- **beautiful Lake Burton**
- **excellent fishing & boating**
- **adjacent to fish hatchery**
- **hiking nearby**
- **closed December 1 through March 15**

At a mere 32 acres you might think Moccasin Creek State Park (elev. 1,866') couldn't compare with North Georgia's other "big" parks, but you would be dead wrong. Located on the wooded shoreline of 2,800-acre Lake Burton and the lush Chattahoochee National Forest, Moccasin Creek is the gateway to a great time. Whether it be boating, fishing, water sports or land adventures such as hiking and camping, Moccasin Creek is a favorite base camp for your mountain adventures.

Accommodations: Generations of campers have been drawn to the park's 55 tent and trailer sites nestled in deep shade beneath towering white pines. Competition for sites is fierce. The campground has an intimate feel to it and each site is just a short walk to the creek or lake.

Picnicking: This is a great park to picnic. An open air pavilion and picnic area alongside the lake provide a perfect setting for this All-American pastime. Parents will also appreciate the playground located here.

Boating: If being on the water is "it" for you - welcome to paradise. Lake Burton with its 62-mile shoreline is a tremendous venue for fishing and recreational boating and skiing. A public boat ramp is available at the fish hatchery adjacent to the park and a private boat dock is available in the park for registered campers.

No boat, no problem. Guests wishing to rent a boat can head just a few miles south along GA 197 to LaPrade's Marina.

Fishing: Splashing Moccasin Creek forms the southern boundary of the park. Guests 11 and younger, or those possessing an honorary license, may fish on this portion of the creek. For everyone else you'll have to head across the highway and fish upstream of the park. You'll definitely need a license and trout stamp - check local regulations carefully before you fish.

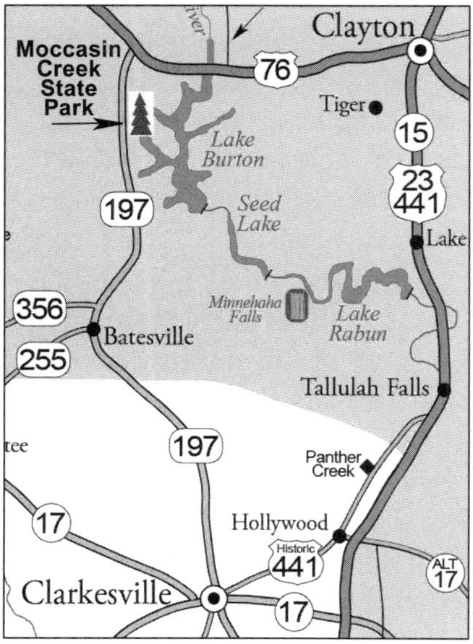

Burton Fish Hatchery: Located just across Moccasin Creek from the park this Georgia Department of Natural Resources facility raises rainbow trout destined for stocking in lakes and streams across North Georgia. Children of all ages will enjoy observing tens of thousands of young trout in various stages of growth. Call the Georgia DNR, Wildlife Resources Division, 706.947.3112 for hours.

Hiking: Need a break from the lake? How about some hiking? Just across the highway from the park is a pleasant 1.2-mile **Nature Loop Trail**. Something a bit more exhilarating? Take the road directly across from the park up to the beautiful 1.5-mile **Hemlock Falls Trail**. This delightful trail follows an old logging bed upstream into the Moccasin Creek watershed. After stretching upstream alongside Moccasin Creek for about one mile, the trail crosses a narrow footbridge over rushing rapids, then continues uphill for several hundred additional yards to pretty Hemlock Falls. Another falls lies about 0.5 miles further up the creek, but you'll have to ford the creek and get precise directions in order to reach it.

Tallulah Gorge State Park #19

One of Georgia's most outstanding landscapes

Tallulah Gorge State Park - Rabun County
338 Jane Hurt Yarn Drive
Tallulah Falls, GA 30573
706.754-7981
www.gastateparks.org
GPS Coordinates:
34.739750°N / 083.395233°W

- **spectacular gorge**
- **5 major waterfalls**
- **great hiking trails**
- **day use area**
- **Jane Hurt Yarn Interpretive Center**
- **Sliding Rock in the bottom of the gorge**

Taking the plunge at Sliding Rock deep in the heart of Tallulah Gorge

One of Georgia's newest parks, Tallulah Gorge State Park has only been around since 1992. Jointly operated by the Georgia Department of Natural Resources and Georgia Power Company, Tallulah Gorge State Park features arguably the most dramatic scenery in Georgia. This spectacular natural chasm is more than 2 miles long and nearly 1,000 feet deep making it one of the deepest canyons east of the Mississippi River.

Carved over time by the relentless waters of the Tallulah River, the gorge features 5 major waterfalls, most of which are easily visible from the park's rim trails. Be sure to check into the history of this fascinating area which was one of the South's great tourist destinations a century ago.

Accommodations: Fifty tent and recreational vehicle sites are available. Call the state park reservation line at 706.754.7979. The park also has a pioneer campground and 3 backcountry adirondack shelters. When there are vacancies they are available on a first-come, first-served basis.

Jane Hurt Yarn Interpretive Center: This is where most everyone begins their Tallulah Gorge experience. This beautiful 16,000-square foot facility contains cultural, historical and natural exhibits dealing with the gorge and surrounding area. Learn all about the Victorian era at Tallulah Falls or enjoy the short feature film which proclaims Tallulah Gorge in all its glory. The center also features a gift shop and information desk where the coveted gorge floor permits are issued.

Terrora Day Use Area: Situated along the wooded shores of 63-acre Tallulah Lake is a picnic pavilion, playground, lakeside picnic tables, hiking/biking trails, a swimming beach, bath house and tennis courts.

Biking Trails: Several options include the easy 1.45-mile (one way) **Shortline Trail** which is flat, paved and shady (the trifecta for novice bikers and young children). The Shortline is located in the Terrora day use area.

Another great biking path is the 5-mile (one way) **Stoneplace Trail** (permit required) which descends from the visitor center to Tugaloo Lake. What goes down must eventually come back up so the trail is rated moderate (some consider it strenuous due to its length). The 4-mile **High Bluff Trail** is a nice option for both hikers and mountain bikers.

Hiking: The park excels in this area, offering something for everyone. One of the easiest and most popular is the aforementioned **Shortline Trail** located in the Terrora day-use section of the park. A portion of this 1.45-mile (one way) paved path follows the restored rail bed of the old Tallulah Falls Railroad. This trail features history, scenery and a dramatic 200' suspension bridge over the Tallulah River. Another easy trail in this part of the park is the 1-mile **Terrora Trail** which begins at the old TF jail and loops around an isolated cove of the lake.

The North and South Rim Trails feature magnificent views of the gorge and several of its trademark waterfalls. Rated easy

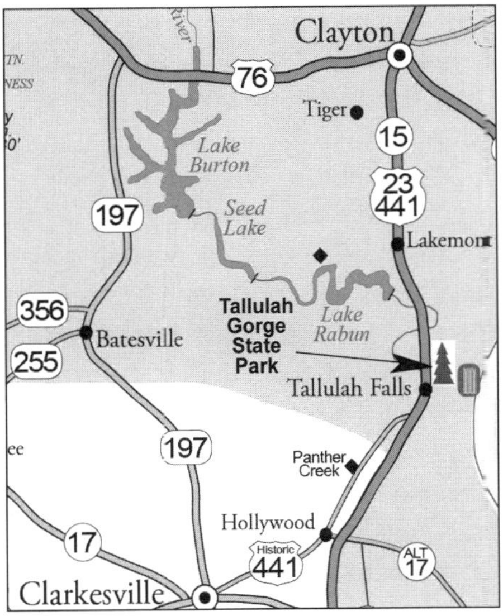

to moderate these trails are about 0.75 mile each and pass a series of stunning overlooks. They begin at the visitor center. A new overlook has recently been added on the north rim about 0.25 mile southeast of Overlook #1. Known as Point Inspiration it requires a moderate 200+' ascent but as the highest overlook along the rim it is well worth the effort. Be sure to obtain a park map at the visitor center - it will help orient you to the trail system.

In order to hike the gorge floor *you must first obtain a permit at the visitor center.* Once you have your permit in hand, either descend the stairway, rock hop across the river and head downstream along the **Gorge Floor Trail,** or descend into the gorge via the wildly steep and rugged **Wallenda Trail** which ends at Sliding Rock, everyone's favorite gorge floor destination. *The gorge floor is dangerous and requires a great deal of stamina to reach and negotiate*, but it's one of Georgia's greatest day hikes.

One of the most dramatic additions to the state park trail system was the spectacular **stairway that descends to the base of Hurricane Falls** deep within the gorge. From the north rim you will descend 310 steps to reach a dramatic suspension bridge perched about 75 feet above the river and the brink of 96' Hurricane Falls.

The tricky river crossing at the base of Hurricane Falls en route to Sliding Rock

To climb back out to the south rim from here takes approximately 345 steps. Going down? From the bridge continue your descent an additional 225 steps to a dramatic observation platform at the base of rugged Hurricane Falls. To go all the way down to the deck and back requires somewhere around 1,150 steps, but who's counting?

Other less dramatic trails include the 5-mile (one way) **Stoneplace Trail** which descends to pretty Lake Tugaloo and the 4-mile **High Bluff Trail** which meanders through the forest adjacent to the visitor center. Both of these trails require permits.

Whitewater Releases: After the damming of Tallulah Lake in 1909, the entire flow of the Tallulah River was diverted through an underground tunnel over one mile in length to the Tallulah hydroelectric plant at the far end of the gorge. In essence the river was "turned off" and the wonderful waterfalls of Tallulah Gorge disappeared.

That all changed with the establishment of the park in 1992. A culvert was inserted through the top of the dam providing a 35-40 cfs (cubic foot per second) water flow through the gorge. This provided a constant water flow that brought the long-silenced falls back to life.

If you really want to see the falls at their pre-dam glory, visit during an aesthetic release; better yet visit the park on one of the handful of whitewater releases in the early spring and fall.

On the first few weekends of both November and April, flood gates atop the dam are opened providing either a 500 cfs or 700 cfs flow. Expert whitewater boaters haul their canoes and kayaks down the stairway over 400 steps to the river and challenge the ominous rapids, including 50' Oceana Falls.

Aesthetic releases: While not quite as dramatic as a whitewater release the regularly scheduled aesthetic releases increase the river's flow about five-fold (about 200 cfs). This increased water flow makes a dramatic difference in the appearance of the majestic waterfalls of Tallulah Gorge.

Kayakers run the flooded gorge during a spring whitewater release.

park map on following page

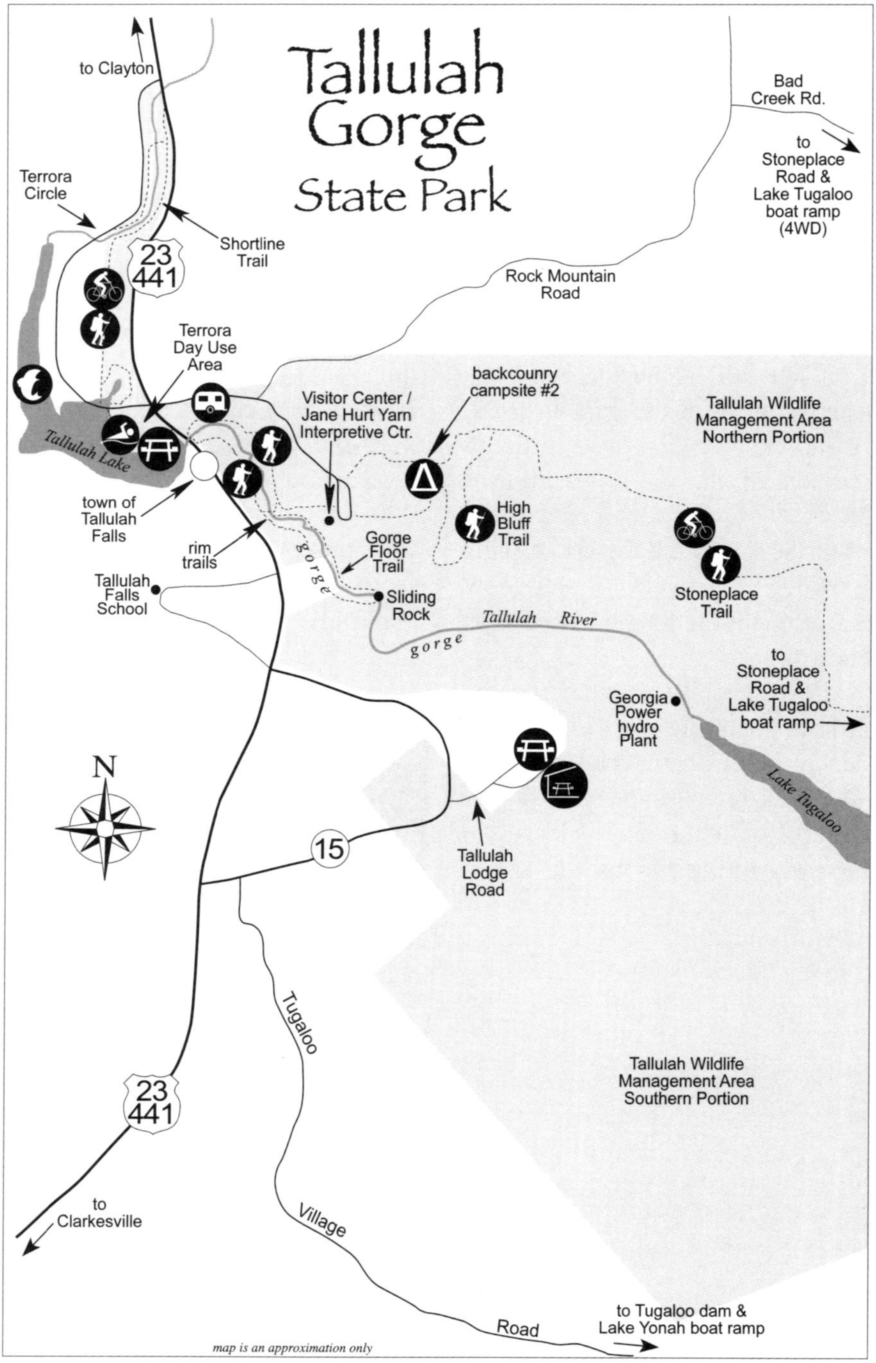
Tallulah Gorge State Park
to Clayton
Terrora Circle
Shortline Trail
23 441
Terrora Day Use Area
Tallulah Lake
town of Tallulah Falls
rim trails
Tallulah Falls School
Visitor Center / Jane Hurt Yarn Interpretive Ctr.
backcounry campsite #2
High Bluff Trail
Gorge Floor Trail
gorge
Sliding Rock
Tallulah River
gorge
Bad Creek Rd.
to Stoneplace Road & Lake Tugaloo boat ramp (4WD)
Rock Mountain Road
Tallulah Wildlife Management Area Northern Portion
Stoneplace Trail
to Stoneplace Road & Lake Tugaloo boat ramp
Georgia Power hydro Plant
Lake Tugaloo
N
15
Tallulah Lodge Road
Tugaloo
Village
Road
Tallulah Wildlife Management Area Southern Portion
23 441
to Clarkesville
to Tugaloo dam & Lake Yonah boat ramp
map is an approximation only

#20 Cloudland Canyon State Park

Dramatic Lookout Mountain canyon and fantastic waterfalls

Cloudland Canyon State Park - Dade County
122 Cloudland Canyon Park Road
Rising Fawn, GA 30738
706.657.4050
www.gastateparks.org
GPS Coordinates:
34.8176°N / 085.4883°W

- **rugged canyon**
- **challenging hikes**
- **2 beautiful waterfalls**
- **beautiful vistas**

The dramatic view of Cloudland Canyon from the West Rim Trail near the Interpretive Center

Beautiful 3,488-acre Cloudland Canyon offers a very different "mountain experience" from the state parks of the central and eastern portion of North Georgia. Cloudland Canyon is actually located on the western edge of Lookout Mountain, and is technically part of the Cumberland plateau. These mountains, unlike their Blue Ridge cousins to the east, feature relatively flat summits and are composed of sandstone and shale dramatically shaped by eons of erosion.

The park is situated around a dramatic gouge in the earth created by Sitton Gulch Creek. The elevations range from just under 2,000 feet up top to about 800 feet at the bottom of the canyon. Hiking ranges from easy rim trails to steep descents into the canyon, and the dramatic topography has created many challenging hiking trails. If you haven't been to Georgia's "other mountains" in a while be sure to plan a visit soon.

Accommodations: The park features 16 cottages and 72 tent, trailer and rv campsites. Hikers will enjoy the 30 walk-in campsites as well as the 11 backcountry campsites. Additional accommodations include a pioneer campground and group lodge which sleeps up to 40.

Picnicking: With all the great scenery along the rim, Cloudland Canyon is a great spot for picnics. The park features 5 picnic shelters which can be reserved and one group shelter which seats 175. There are plenty of single picnic tables scattered about the rim as well.

Hiking: Cloudland Canyon State Park offers a great variety of trails but because of the dramatic geology of the park most are rated moderate to strenuous.

The easiest is the 0.6-mile **Overlook Trail** which follows the rim from the main parking area to a series of north and east facing overlooks. Rated easy to moderate.

The 2.5-mile **Backcountry Loop Trail** offers a very enjoyable hike. Rated moderate, this trail features seasonal wildflowers and deep woods.

The popular **Waterfalls Trail** is approximately 2 miles round trip and rated strenuous. This steep trail features stairs - lots of stairs - you'll cover over 1,200 in your trip down and back up. The payoff is two beautiful waterfalls at the bottom: the creatively named waterfall #1 (90') and waterfall #2 (60').

Next up is the 5-mile **West Rim Loop Trail**. Park literature describes this trail as "one of the most scenic hiking trails in the nation" and they may well be right. The trail begins at the Daniel Creek bridge and features great views of Cloudland Canyon, Trenton and nearby Sand Mountain. This trail is rated moderate to strenuous.

The longest of Cloudland Canyon's State Park trails is the 6.5-mile **Sitton's Gulch Loop Trail**. No bones about it, this trail is rated strenuous and for good reason. The trail follows Daniel Creek through fragrant hemlocks and features several nice cascading small waterfalls. There are several steep grades along the way not to mention the 600 or so steps required both at the beginning and end of the hike.

Be sure to talk to park representatives for a more thorough description of these trails. These trails are challenging - don't attempt something beyond your limits.

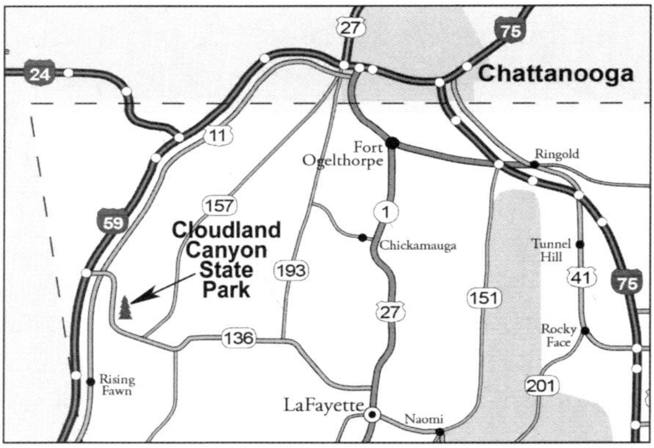

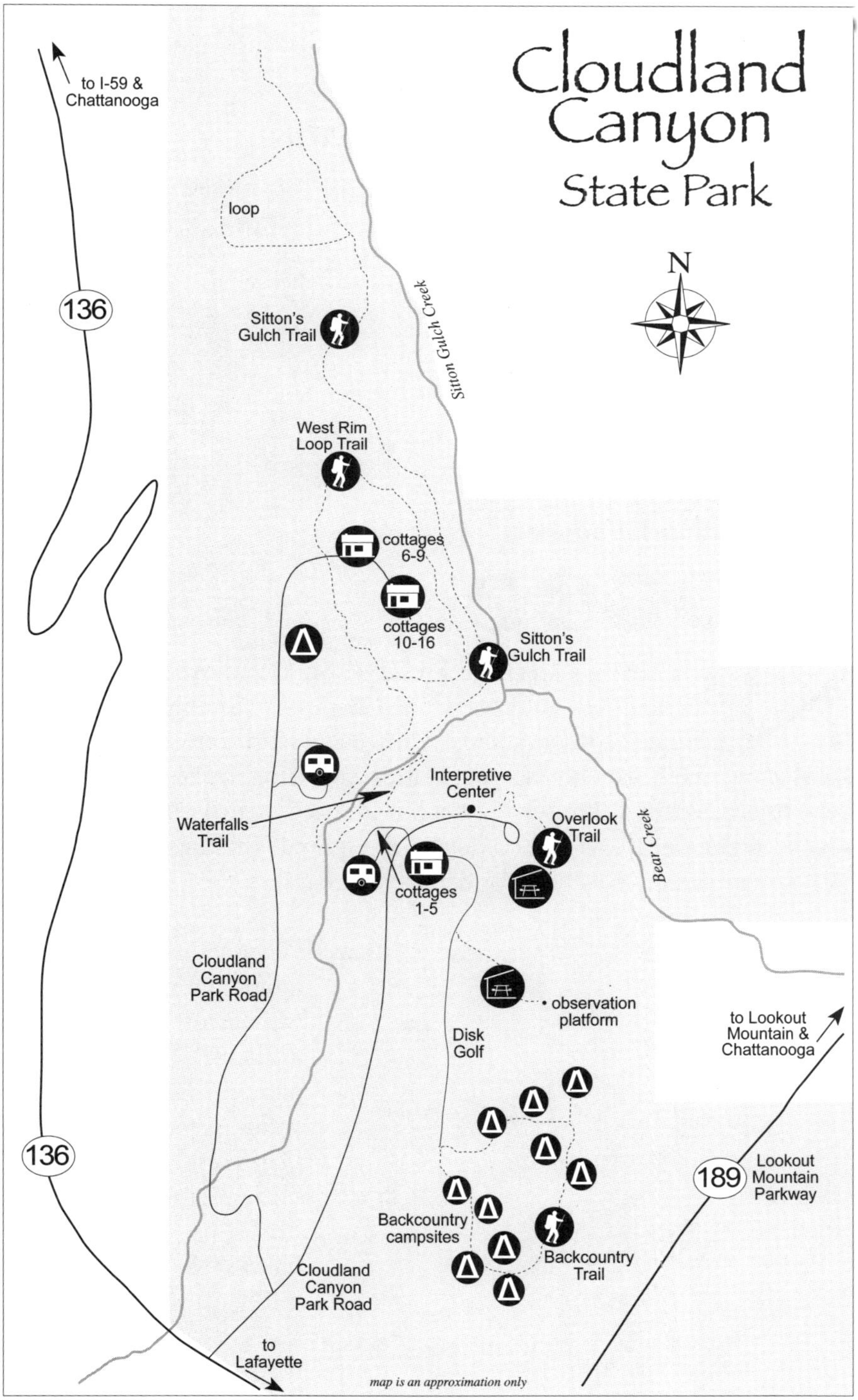
Cloudland Canyon State Park
N
to I-59 & Chattanooga
136
loop
Sitton's Gulch Trail
Sitton Gulch Creek
West Rim Loop Trail
cottages 6-9
cottages 10-16
Sitton's Gulch Trail
Interpretive Center
Waterfalls Trail
Overlook Trail
Bear Creek
cottages 1-5
Cloudland Canyon Park Road
observation platform
Disk Golf
to Lookout Mountain & Chattanooga
136
189
Lookout Mountain Parkway
Backcountry campsites
Backcountry Trail
Cloudland Canyon Park Road
to Lafayette
map is an approximation only

Smithgall Woods State Park #21

Trophy trout stream and wildlife preserve

Smithgall Woods State Park - White County
61 Tsalaki Trail
Helen, GA 30545
706.878.3087
www.gastateparks.org
GPS Coordinates:
34.691950°N / 083.767150°W

- **"catch and release" trophy trout stream**
- **walking & hiking**
- **bicycling**
- **beautiful cottages**
- **trail to Dukes Creek Falls**
- **educational programs**

Now a Georgia Heritage Preserve, Smithgall Woods State Park was acquired in 1994 from Charles A. Smithgall, Jr., noted Georgia conservationist and successful businessman. This spectacular 5,604-acre preserve features sparkling Dukes Creek as its centerpiece. While fishing is big here, it is strictly catch-and-release with special regulations, and reservations are required. Hunting is big here as well - visit the park's website for details and dates.

Accommodations: The park markets its accommodations as an "elegant mountain retreat" and 5 wonderful cottages are available. There is also a pioneer campground for youth groups available. (The park is also a perfect setting for a wedding.)

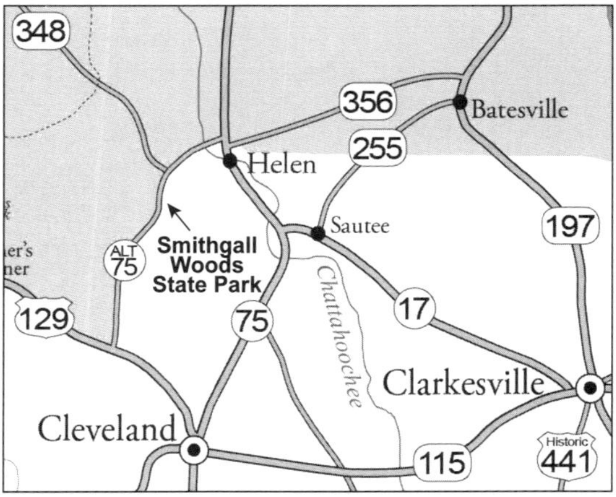

Hiking & Biking: Four miles of splendid hiking trails and 18 miles of roads lace the expansive compound providing plenty of room for visitors to spread out and explore this fascinating preserve. The easiest path is the 0.3-mile **Visitor Center Trail.** The 1.6-mile **Laurel Ridge Loop** Trail also begins at the visitor center and features a nice winter view of nearby Mt. Yonah. Other trails on the property include the 1.5-mile **Ash Creek Trail**, the 0.5-mile **Cathy Ellis Trail,** the 0.55-mile **Wetland Loop Trail,** and the 0.9-mile **Martin's Mine Loop Trail**. Obtain a detailed park map and carefully plan your walking adventure.

Wildlife: Wildlife lovers will enjoy visiting the planted food crop areas on the property. These areas attract a wide variety of wildlife including whitetail deer which are abundant in the area. Viewing stands have been constructed allowing visitors the opportunity to observe native species in their natural environment.

Picnicking: Four picnic shelters are available to accommodate groups or individuals. Three of these are located along sparkling Dukes Creek.

Odds & Ends: Shuttle service and guided tours are normally available but only on certain days of the week. Visitors desiring these services should call ahead and enquire about schedule and availability. Be sure to stop at the visitor center to begin your Smithgall Woods experience. This is a large park with a vast network of confusing roads and trails. Visitors must register before launching into the park.

Location: From Helen take GA 17/75 north for 1.5 miles. Turn left onto GA 75 ALT and drive 3 miles. The park is on the left just beyond the Richard Russell Scenic Highway.

Visitors should obtain an official park map for reference purposes.

James H. (Sloppy) Floyd State Park #22

Peaceful setting on two beautiful lakes

James H. (Sloppy) Floyd State Park - Chattooga County
2800 Sloppy Floyd Lake Road
Summerville, GA 30747
706.857.0826
www.gastateparks.org
GPS Coordinates:
34.4399°N / 083.3372°W

- **2 fishing lakes**
- **hiking trails**
- **great picnicking**
- **easy access to 60-mile Pinhoti Trail**
- **camping**

James H. (Sloppy) Floyd State Park isn't exactly cast in the same mold as other Georgia state parks located "in the mountains," but if you find yourself in the northwest corner of the state you really should stop and check-out this pretty 561-acre park. The park is named for Rep. James H. "Sloppy" Floyd who served in the Georgia House of Representatives from 1953 to 1974.

The park is located at the southwestern tip of Georgia's Chattahoochee National Forest in a serene rural setting. This park is perfect for slowing down and taking it easy. Just a few cottages and a couple dozen camping sites set among 2 pretty lakes are ideal for wetting a hook, taking a pedal-boat for a spin or serving as a backdrop for a picnic.

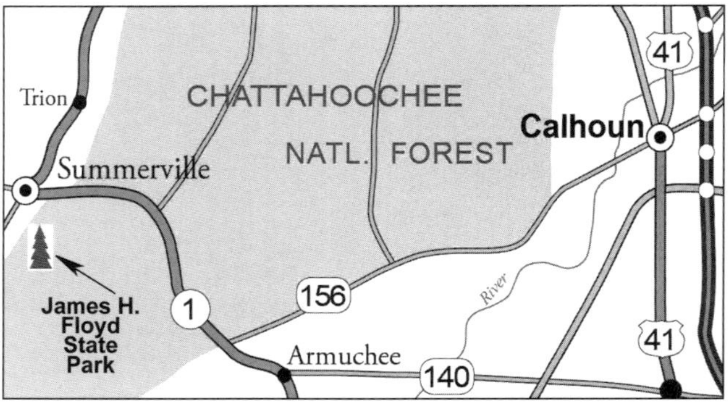

Accommodations: Four cottages are available as well as 25 tent, trailer and recreational vehicle campsites.

Lake: Undoubtedly the centerpiece of this idyllic park is the lake, actually 2 lakes. Creatively referred to as Upper Lake (16 acres) and Lower Lake (34 acres), these two gems provide a great medium for canoes, rowboats or electric powered boats. One of the nicest features is an extended boardwalk which stretches across Upper Lake providing a great fishing platform. Plenty of good picnic shelters and tables are scattered around the lakes as well.

Hiking: The 3-mile **Lake Loop Trail** is very popular. This path circles both lakes and is rated *easy.*

The popular **Marble Mine Trail** can be hiked a variety of ways with distances ranging from about 1.6 to 2.2 miles total. Refer to an official park map to plan your route. The trail is a combination of wide gravel roads and footpaths that reach back to the dramatic entrance of an old marble mine and features a small pond and boardwalk at the yawning mine entrance.

The 240-mile **Pinhoti Trail** can be accessed from the park as well. This path is actually the longest trail in Georgia (140 miles). Georgia's portion begins at the Alabama line in Polk County and heads northwest to its junction with the Benton MacKaye Trail (portions of the Pinhoti requires walking along roads for now).

Just north of the southern park entrance is a Pinhoti Trail parking area. The 1.6-mile **Pinhoti Access Trail** reaches east to a junction with the Pinhoti Trail.

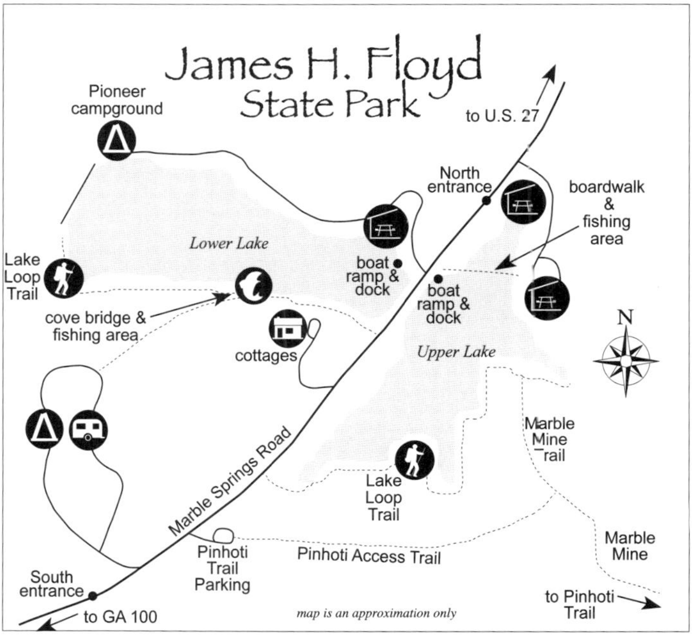

3

North Georgia's FALLING WATERS

Anna Ruby Falls #23

One of Georgia's most popular waterfalls is a twin

Anna Ruby Falls Scenic Area
Chattooga Ranger District
Chattahoochee National Forest
706.878.3574
GPS coordinates:
34.757640°N / 83.710190°W

- **gorgeous twin waterfall**
- **interpretive trail**
- **creekside picnic area**
- **visitor center/gift shop**
- **adjacent to Unicoi State Park**
- **USFS fee area**

Anna Ruby Falls should be at the top of anyone's North Georgia bucket list. This rare twin cascade occurs at the junction of York and Curtis Creeks, their waters mingling at the base to form scenic Smith Creek, the major feeder stream for Unicoi Lake. The waterfall is named for Anna Ruby Nichols, the only daughter of Col. John H. Nichols, an early landowner and builder of the magnificent Victorian home *West End,* directly across GA 17 from the Nacoochee Indian Mound south of Helen.

1,600-acre Anna Ruby Falls Scenic Area was established in 1964 and quickly became a favorite North Georgia destination. The 0.4-mile interpretive trail leading from the visitor center to the base of the falls is a pleasure to traverse. The path is paved and features a slight incline (except for one short moderate steep section). Several benches have been strategically placed along the path if you need to catch your breath. The trail crosses tumbling Smith Creek over a beautiful footbridge and interpretive plaques describe various natural points of interest along the way.

A series of boardwalks and observation platforms have been constructed near the base of the falls providing several excellent vantage points. This is a great spot to linger and not surprisingly hundreds do just that. On crowded summer and fall weekends you may have to wait your turn to get a photo at an open spot along the railing.

As you face the falls, Curtis Creek tumbles 153' down a steep exposed rock face into a shallow boulder-filled pool. To the right York Creek free-falls about 50 feet. At this point on the southern shoulders of lofty Tray mountain the two streams merge in a beautiful symphony of sights, sounds and fragrances of falling water.

The Cradle of Forestry Interpretive Association operates a gift shop under special permit from the U.S. Forest Service. The gift shop offers a nice selection of books, maps, souvenirs and snacks. Just outside the visitor center is a large deck overlooking a small pool on Smith Creek. Huge trout can often be observed waiting for their next meal.

Picnicking: A scenic picnic area is located across Smith Creek adjacent to the visitor center parking lot. Fourteen picnic tables are located alongside the tumbling stream.

Hiking: In addition to the 0.4-mile path to Anna Ruby Falls the 0.1-mile **Lion's Eye Trail** has been developed for persons with visual impairments. This paved path features a cable which is used as a handrail guiding visitors from one interpretive plaque to the next. The plaques have been produced in braille as well as English. The 4.6-mile **Smith Creek Trail** connects the waterfall with Unicoi State Park. Ironically, this moderate trail doesn't access its namesake creek until it reaches Anna Ruby Falls.

Directions: From Helen drive north on GA 17/75 for 1.1 miles. Turn right onto GA 356 and proceed 1.4 miles. Veer left onto FS 242 and drive 3.5 miles to the Anna Ruby Falls Scenic Area. Note: you will pass a Unicoi State Park kiosk; if you are not stopping in the park you are not required to pay the admission fee. However, you will have to pay at the USFS kiosk at the entrance to the Anna Ruby Falls Scenic Area just a bit further up the road. It can be a little confusing.

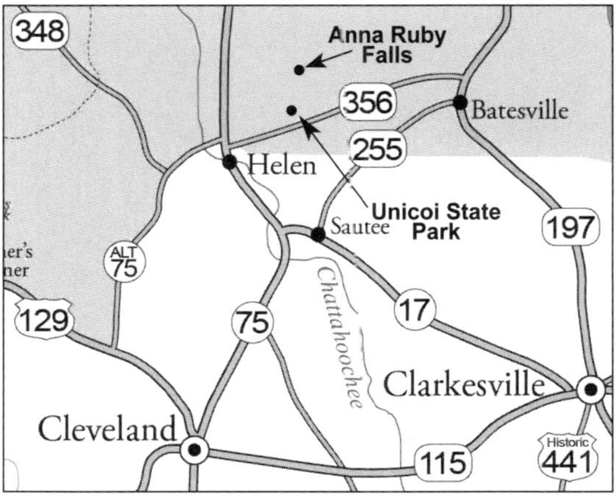

Dukes Creek Falls #24

Energetic walk to the base of this alluring cascade and stream

Dukes Creek Scenic Area
Chattooga Ranger District
Chattahoochee National Forest
706.754.6221
GPS coordinates:
34.703259°N / 83.788547°W

- **beautiful cascade**
- **long range view from parking area**
- **fantastic boardwalk and viewing platform at base**
- **trout fishing**
- **USFS fee area**

Platform above Dukes Creek.

Scenic Duke's Creek Falls gives viewers 2 options: you can either view the upper portion from afar or get up-close and personal. A looping 1.1-mile (one way) trail descends from the parking area to a magnificent boardwalk and observation decks across from the 200' cascade (which is actually on Davis Creek). The cascading stream below the platform is Dodd Creek and it is in perpetual motion. When the 2 creeks merge they become Dukes Creek. Easy, huh? The total change in elevation is around 400' so if climbing hills is not your thing you can get a rather long range view (approximately 300 yards) from the boardwalk adjacent to the parking lot. Dukes Creek gorge at the base of the waterfall is extraordinarily scenic - it's a great place to linger, and the trout fishing isn't too bad here either.

Directions: From Helen drive north on GA 17/75 for 1.5 miles. Turn left onto GA 75 ALT and drive 2.3 miles to GA 348 (Russell Scenic Hwy) on the right. Drive 2 miles to the parking area.

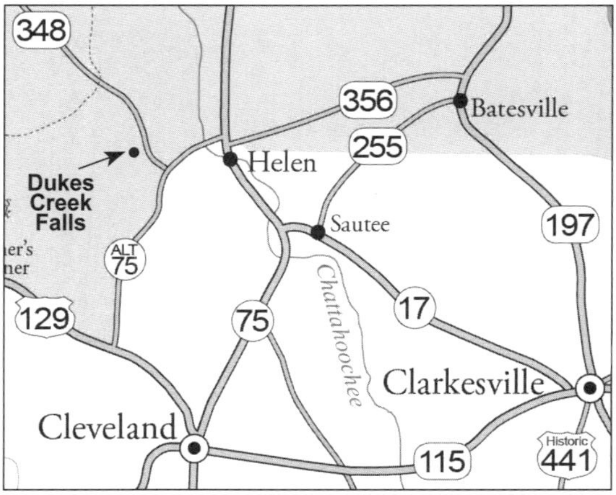

#25 Horsetrough Falls

Beautiful cascade near the Chattahoochee headwaters

Upper Chattahoochee Campground
Chattooga Ranger District
Chattahoochee National Forest
706.754.6221
GPS coordinates:
34.795093°N / 83.788234°W

- **very short walk**
- **observation platform**
- **beautiful camping area**
- **trout fishing**
- **USFS fee area**

Water level makes all the difference here as Horsetrough Creek is a fairly small stream. When the water is up this is one of North Georgia's prettiest waterfalls. The drive will take much longer than the walk as the shortest route is just under 5 miles (one way) on a winding Forest Service road. If you can handle a flat 200-yard walk you can view this waterfall. Pay attention to the small stream you cross via a wooden footbridge as you stroll to Horsetrough - it's the Chattahoochee River on it's way to Atlanta and ultimately the Gulf of Mexico. Take your time, have a picnic, then take scenic FS 44 back to Helen, much of it along the river.

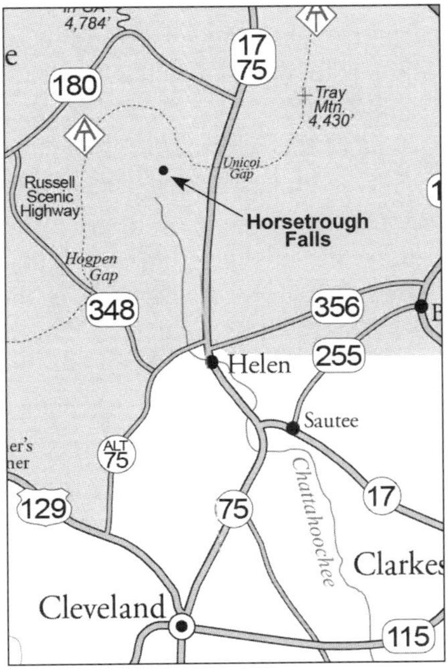

Directions: From the Chattahoochee River bridge in Helen drive north on GA 17/75 for 9.4 miles. Turn left onto FS 44 and drive 4.75 miles to FS 44F (Upper Chattahoochee River campground). To reach the trailhead drive to the far end of the camping loop. See page 110 for an additional route.

The Falls of High Shoals #26

Beautiful series of falls on sparkling High Shoals Creek

High Shoals Scenic Area
Chattooga Ranger District
Chattahoochee National Forest
706.754.6221
GPS coordinates:
34.825649°N / 83.723230°W

- **series of waterfalls**
- **500' change in elevation**
- **road can be difficult**
- **Appalachian Trail nearby**

Blue Hole Falls

Two beautiful but distinctively different waterfalls are hidden deep within 170-acre High Shoals Scenic Area near Unicoi Gap in Towns County. A well-worn blue-blazed hiking path descends nearly 500 vertical feet over its 1.2-mile length. A long looping series of switchbacks makes the grade a bit more forgiving but it's definitely not an easy hike. Just remember it's all downhill to the falls; the really fun part is the steady uphill walk back to the parking area.

At the base of the switchbacks the trail crosses High Shoals Creek over a narrow footbridge, then negotiates several hundred yards of relatively flat terrain before descending again, this time along an old road bed which parallels the creek. Turn left onto a prominent side trail and follow the sound of falling water to Blue Hole Falls.

Gorgeous 15' **Blue Hole Falls** plunges into a deep rocky pool, hence the name. The Forest Service has constructed an observation platform across the pool from the falls that offers a perfect view. Though you can often find visitors swimming in the pool or even jumping from the top of the falls into the pool, resist the urge to do so. There have been dozens of injuries and several fatalities on these waterfalls.

Retrace your steps to the main trail, turn left and continue your descent along the old road bed. At about the 1.1 mile mark the trail is somewhat blocked, effectively turning the path sharply left and onto a side trail which descends several hundred yards to the base of **High Shoals Falls**. High Shoals is definitely the higher of the two falls checking in at around 100'. It begins as a narrow flume then spreads across the cliff in a chaotic, disorganized descent into a jumble of boulders at the base.

High Shoals Falls features its own observation deck at the base. This is really the only safe point to observe the waterfall. It is common to see people boulder-hopping on the slippery rocks in and around the creek; it is also common to see them falling on their tails. Even worse, on more than one occasion I've seen individuals high on the cliff face at the edge of the falls. This stunt belongs in the "one slip, you're dead" category.

You might also remember that like most of the falls in North Georgia, High Shoals occurs on a fairly small creek. During periods of drought the falls will be greatly diminished. Winter and early spring are the best seasons to visit High Shoals. Be sure to allow yourself enough daylight for the climb back out of the gorge.

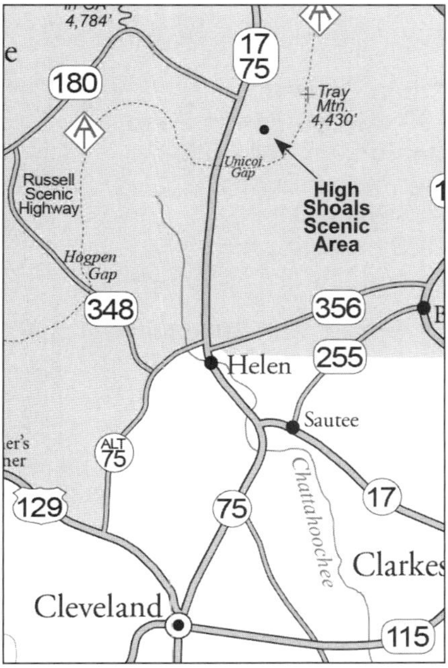

Directions: From the Chattahoochee River bridge in Helen drive north on GA 17/75 for approximately 11.5 miles (about 2 miles past Unicoi Gap). Watch for FS 283 (Indian Grave Gap Road) on the right - it can be hard to spot and requires a sharp right turn. In the first few hundred yards you'll splash through the shallow Hiawassee River (really just a creek), then continue 1.3 bumpy miles to a small parking area on the left. If the sign is missing look for a small green trail marker (#19).

rugged High Shoals Falls

Cane Creek Falls #27

Beautiful cascade on the grounds of Camp Glisson

Camp Glisson
690 Camp Glisson Road
Dahlonega, GA 30533
www.glisson.org
706.864.6181
GPS coordinates:
34.554259°N / 83.008244°W

- **beautiful 30' cascade**
- **easy short stroll**
- **very close to town**
- **remember you are a guest here**

Say you're in historic Dahlonega and you want to see some falling water, but you don't have much time. Problem solved. Take the 5-minute drive out to Camp Glisson. If camp isn't in session you can view beautiful Cane Creek Falls. This ministry of the North Georgia Conference of United Methodists graciously allows visitors to walk down and view their waterfall when it doesn't interfere with their main job, which is running a camp. Unfortunately for visitors this could be most of the summer. This surprisingly large waterfall can be viewed from a platform above the brink or from the stream bank several hundred feet downstream of the waterfall. When you visit, please be on your best behavior and as the old saying goes, "take only photos, leave only footprints."

Directions:
From downtown Dahlonega proceed north on GA 60 Business Spur for 2 miles. Veer left onto Cane Creek Road and proceed 0.8 mile to the camp visitor center. Be sure to ask permission to view the waterfall.

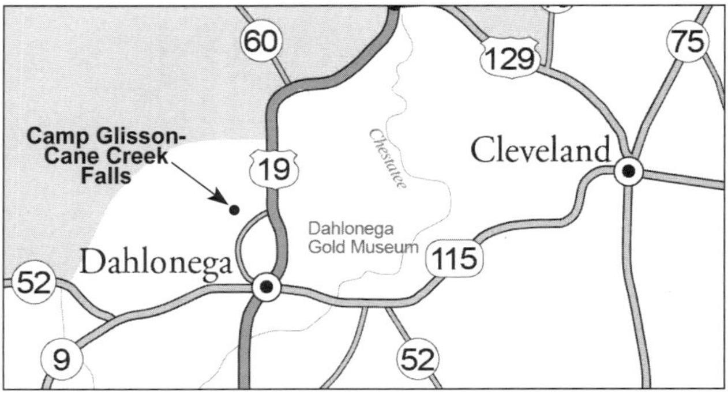

#28 Dick's Creek Falls

Roadside waterfall on one of Georgia's favorite trout streams

Dick's Creek Falls on Waters Creek

Blue Ridge Ranger District
Chattahoochee National Forest
706.745.6928
GPS coordinates:
34.67950°N / 83.93702°W

- **trophy trout stream (note special regulations)**
- **easy access**
- **parking lot and restrooms across the road**

Located along splashing Waters Creek, one of North Georgia's finest trophy trout streams, this roadside waterfall is quite easy to view. The waterfall is just below the confluence with Dick's Creek, hence the name. From U.S. 19 proceed 2.8 miles along FS 34. The waterfall is visible from the road as you approach the parking area. There is a USFS parking lot with toilet just across the road from the waterfall.

Dick's Creek Falls is a popular hangout for both locals and tourists during the hot summer months. The large pool downstream of the waterfall is a heavily-frequented swimming hole and trout fishermen are pretty fond of it as well. There area some scenic chutes and shoals above the waterfall also but be very careful if you venture onto the slick rocks, as you wouldn't want to fall in and "swim" Dick's Creek Falls just a few yards downstream.

If you're hungry for more falling water continue 2 additional miles up FS 34 to a low-water bridge on Blood Mountain Creek. Park and walk across the creek then continue on a primitive path upstream to several small cascades.

Directions: Waters Creek is located about 12 miles north of Dahlonega. Follow U.S. 19 and turn onto Dick's Creek Road (FS 34). Proceed 2.8 miles to the parking area on the right.

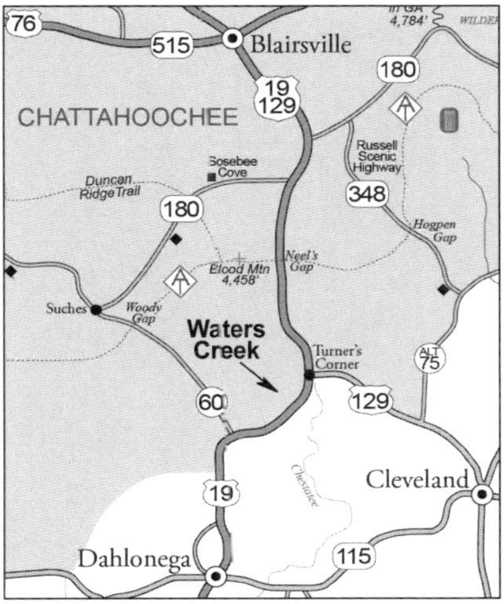

Helton Creek Falls #29

Beautiful waterfall is short drive from Vogel State Park

Blue Ridge Ranger District
Chattahoochee National Forest
706.745.6928
GPS coordinates:
34.752591°N / 83.895741°W

- **2 separate cascades**
- **easy short stroll**
- **beautiful setting**
- **good spot for streamside picnic**

The most difficult thing about experiencing Helton Creek Falls is enduring the 2 miles of bumpy gravel road that is known as FS 118. Actually it's not *that* bad but keep your eyes open for potholes. Helton Creek is one of Georgia's prettiest waterfalls and it receives heavy visitation, especially on warm-weather weekends. This 60' beauty, perched at an altitude of 2,221', slides down an exposed cliff into one of Georgia's most scenic plunge pools. Surrounded by laurel and rhododendron the scene is quite beautiful. Visitors will pass a second, much smaller waterslide as they make the short climb to Helton Creek Falls' wooden observation deck. Visitors often explore along the exposed rocks alongside the lower drop but be careful as it is very slippery here.

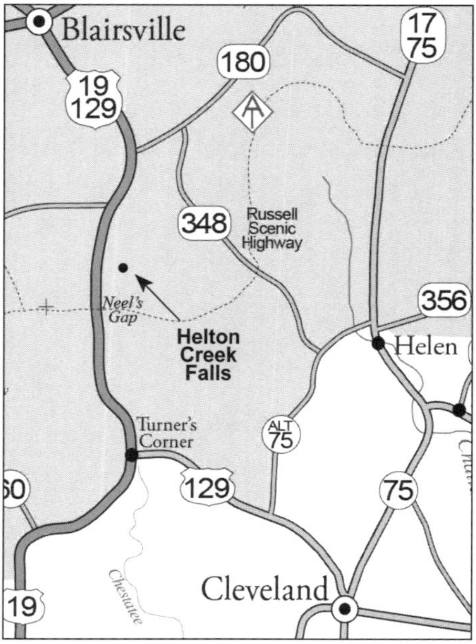

Directions: From Neel's Gap on U.S. 19/129 drive north for 1.6 miles. Turn right onto Helton Creek Road (FS 118). The pavement will soon turn to gravel. Follow the road for 2.3 bumpy miles to the Helton Creek Falls parking area on the right.

7/4/14 Chris Erin Davis

#30 Amicalola Falls

Get up close and personal with Georgia's highest cascade

Amicalola Falls State Park
240 Amicalola Falls State Park Road
Dawsonville, GA 30534
706.265.4703
www.gastateparks.org
GPS coordinates:
34.5962089°N / 83.3598863°W

- **729' total drop**
- **multiple viewing locations**
- **upper portions visible from the base**
- **park entrance fee required**

Amicalola Falls is one of those rare North Georgia destinations that actually rates a second mention. The park is described in greater detail beginning on page 21, but the waterfall is worthy as a destination all on its own. The waterfall is officially listed as 729' which is good enough to make it one of the highest in the eastern U.S., but really only the uppermost several hundred feet are able to be viewed easily or safely. The name *Amicalola* is from a native American word meaning "tumbling waters" and this cascade certainly lives up to its name.

There are several ways to view Amicalola. You can take the easy route to the upper cascades via the West Ridge Falls Access Trail (handicap accessible). It accesses a wooden footbridge below the open upper cascades. You can also get a partial view from the reflection pool, or, better yet, combine a workout with your waterfall viewing by taking the Appalachian Trail Approach Trail from the reflection pool up to the footbridge.

Directions: Amicalola Falls State Park is located on GA 52 approximately 20 miles west of Dahlonega.

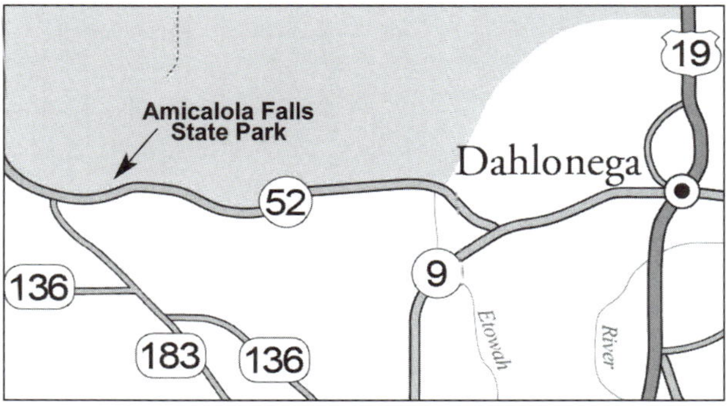

Toccoa Falls #31

One of Georgia's rare free-falling waterfalls

Toccoa Falls College
107 N. Chapel Drive
Toccoa Falls, GA 30598
706.886.7299 • www.tfc.edu
GPS coordinates:
34.5962089°N / 83.3598863°W

- **Gate Cottage gift shop and restaurant**
- **easy short path**
- **nominal entrance fee**

Beautiful Toccoa Falls is one of a handful of major North Georgia waterfalls that actually free-falls almost its entire height. The majority of Georgia's major waterfalls cascade for most or all of their length but this 186' drop, touted as "higher than Niagara," launches from a point high atop a massive brown cliff into thin air. The name is derived from the Cherokee word *Toccoah* which has been translated "beautiful."

Interestingly the waterfall really isn't in an area you would consider "the mountains." Toccoa is located in the foothills of North Georgia on the edge of a feature known as the Tallulah dome. The elevation at the falls (1,020') is around 500' less than the closest towns of Cornelia and Clarkesville, which are only about 12 miles away.

Toccoa Falls College maintains a gentle gravel walkway that stretches several hundred yards along Toccoa Creek up to the viewing area at the base of a massive boulder-lined plunge pool. The pathway passes a memorial commemorating the 1977 dam break and flood that killed 39 students, staff and family members at the college.

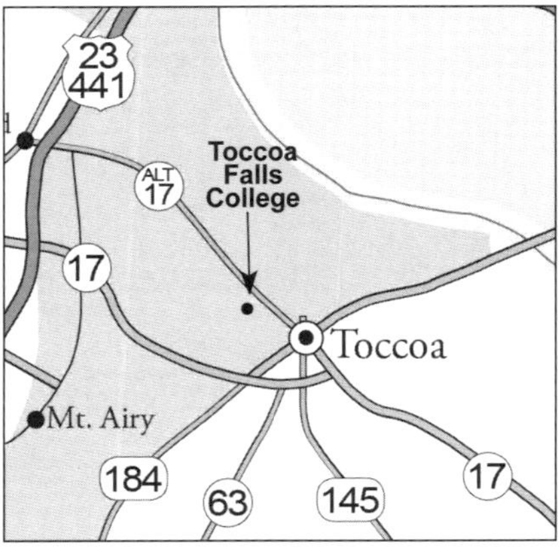

Directions: Toccoa Falls College is located just north of Toccoa on GA 17 ALT. Turn into the college and proceed to the stop sign. Go straight following the signs to the Gate Cottage.

#32 Panther Creek Falls

Surprisingly large waterfall at the end of a beautiful hike

Panther Creek Recreation Area
Chattooga Ranger District
Chattahoochee National Forest
706.754.6221
GPS coordinates:
34.768199°N / 83.398803°W

- **7 miles round trip**
- **picnicking**
- **trout fishing**
- **seasonal wildflowers abound**
- **primitive camping at the falls**
- **USFS fee area**

The 3.5-mile (one way) Panther Creek Trail is one of the most popular day hikes in northeast Georgia. This path has everything you could wish for: a rushing stream, beautiful forest setting, interesting geology, and a gorgeous 75' stair-stepping waterfall as the primary destination.

Hikers pass an extended series of scenic shoals at the 2.5 mile mark, but don't mistake these for the waterfall. When you arrive at Panther Creek Falls the trail will be forced over and around a large stream-blocking rock outcrop and the unmistakable sound of falling water fills the air. The trail descends steeply and pauses at a popular primitive camping area adjacent to an expansive plunge pool at the base of the cascade. Be aware that this is a very popular destination during the peak season and there may be scores of visitors swarming the waterfall. Plan your trip wisely and you may have the area all to yourself. Note: there are portions of the trail that have steep drop-offs and tricky rock overhangs. Use caution!

Directions: From the U.S. 441 bridge in Tallulah Falls proceed south for 2.3 miles. Turn right onto Old Historic 441 and drive 1.5 miles to the Panther Creek Recreation Area on the right.

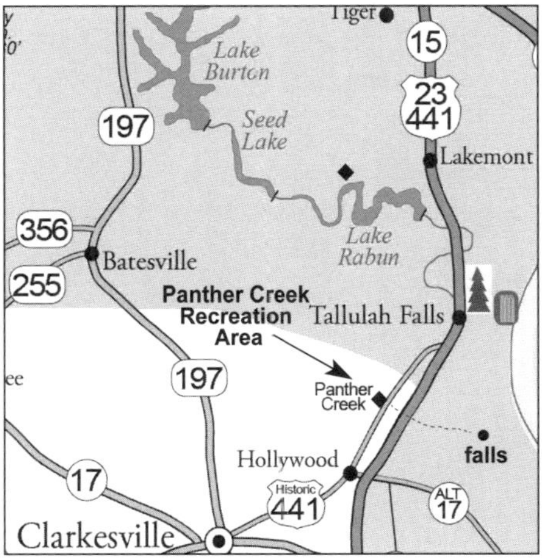

Minnehaha Falls #33

This secluded waterfall just may be Georgia's prettiest cascade

Chattooga Ranger District
Chattahoochee National Forest
706.754.6221
GPS coordinates:
34.760799°N / 83.501800°W

- **easy short walk**
- **nice picnic spot (no tables though)**
- **convenient to Rabun Beach Recreation Area**

Arguably one of the most underrated waterfalls in North Georgia, beautiful Minnehaha Falls is located at the end of a short 0.3-mile footpath along Lake Rabun's secluded western shoreline. The waterfall occurs on the appropriately-named Fall Creek. Here Minnehaha tumbles about 60' over dozens of horizontal ledges. The creek pauses momentarily at the base then continues over yet another cascade just downstream. The viewing area is small but a large rock slab at the base of the waterfall makes a natural bench and vantage point. This is a picturesque setting especially in the late spring and summer when the laurel and rhododendron are blooming. Don't disturb the vegetation or climb the banks around the waterfall; the area is heavily visited and shows some wear. Note: do not try to climb this waterfall - it is extremely dangerous!

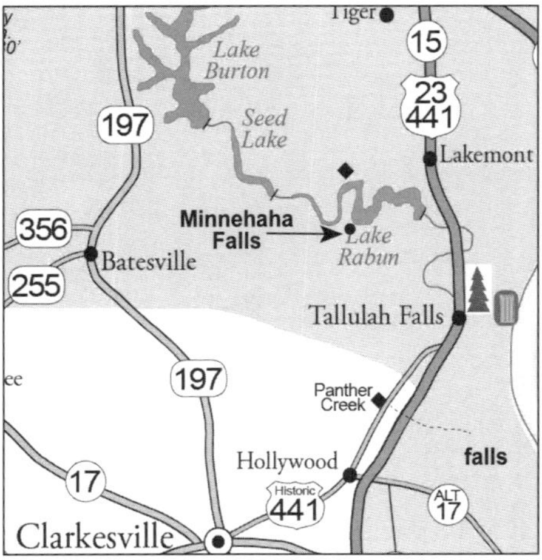

Directions: Follow the directions on page 113 to Rabun Beach Recreation Area. Continue an additional 1.7 miles and turn left onto Low Gap Road, crossing a low water bridge over the Tallulah River directly below Seed Lake dam. Proceed .15 miles and bear left onto Bear Gap Road. Follow Bear Gap Road for 1.6 miles to a small gravel pull-off on the left.

#34 Wildcat Creek Sliding Rock

A short daring slide into an icy plunge pool

Chattooga Ranger District
Chattahoochee National Forest
706.754.6221
GPS coordinates:
34.83344°N / 83.60650°W

- **15' waterslide**
- **roadside**
- **fishing**
- **USFS camping closeby**

Some waterfalls you visit because you want to witness and enjoy their incredible natural beauty; then there are some that you visit because of *what you can do at that waterfall*. The falls on Wildcat Creek, better known as Sliding Rock, is just that kind of place. It's not a big waterfall but come summertime it becomes a popular destination for hardy souls who brave the icy waters for a short but thrilling trip into a broad plunge pool. Just be aware this is not Six Flags and there are definitely risks to venturing out onto the top of a waterfall, even a small one. There have been injuries here so do be careful if you decide to join this particular club of adventurers. You may even have a few trout fishermen competing for use of the plunge pool as this is a popular trout stream, so don't get too crazy.

West Wildcat Creek Road is an extremely scenic drive as it follows Wildcat Creek upstream, and there are a few smaller cascades immediately downstream of Sliding Rock that you may wish to view while you are here.

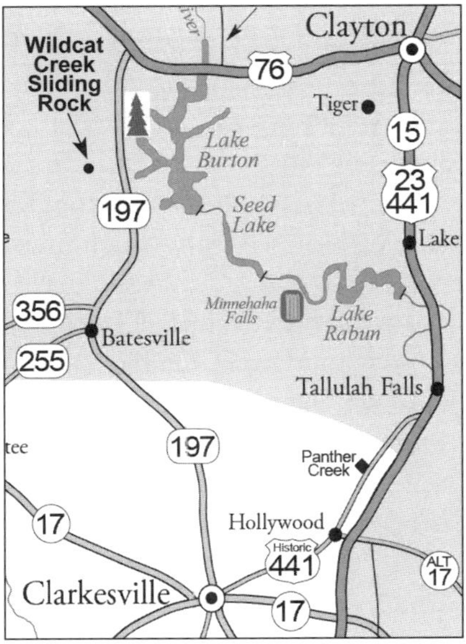

Directions: From Clayton take U.S. 76 west for 11 miles. Turn left (south) onto GA 197 and drive 5 miles to West Wildcat Road (FS 127) on the right) about 1.4 miles south of Moccasin Creek State Park. Drive 1.4 miles on the narrow gravel road to Sliding Rock.

Dick's Creek Falls #35

Pretty waterfall plunges directly into the Chattooga River

Chattooga Ranger District
Chattahoochee National Forest
706.754.6221
GPS coordinates:
34.873056°N / 83.255278°W

- **50' waterslide**
- **0.5 mile (one way)**
- **Bartram and Chattooga River Trail network**
- **close to Sandy Ford**

Wilderness waterfalls make enticing destinations, but with no observation decks or railings visitors must use good judgement and common sense. If this describes you, give Dick's Creek Falls a visit. The most direct route requires an easy half-mile stroll and begins at the Dick's Creek ford on Sandy Ford Road. Follow the trail into the woods and continue 0.4 mile to an intersection with the Bartram Trail. Continue straight ahead and follow a spur trail alongside Dick's Creek to the top of the rugged 50' waterfall (aka Five Finger Falls).

The waterfall slides directly into the Chattooga River in a dramatic left-hand bend in the river featuring Dick's Creek Ledge, a Class IV whitewater drop. The path passes within a few yards of the exposed brink of the falls so stay well back from the edge. Continue down the main path and drop to the river's edge for a good look back at the waterfall from below.

An alternate route is to drive across the Dick's Creek ford and continue uphill to the Bartram Trail crossing. Park here and walk north. The path soon merges with the Chattooga River Trail and continues 0.5 mile to the side path on the right which follows Dick's Creek to the waterfall.

Directions: From Clayton take Warwoman Road (at the Days Inn) east for 5.6 miles. Turn right onto Sandy Ford Road. Proceed 0.65 mile and make a sharp left, crossing Warwoman Creek. Proceed .4 miles along the gravel road to the Dick's Creek ford. Park here.

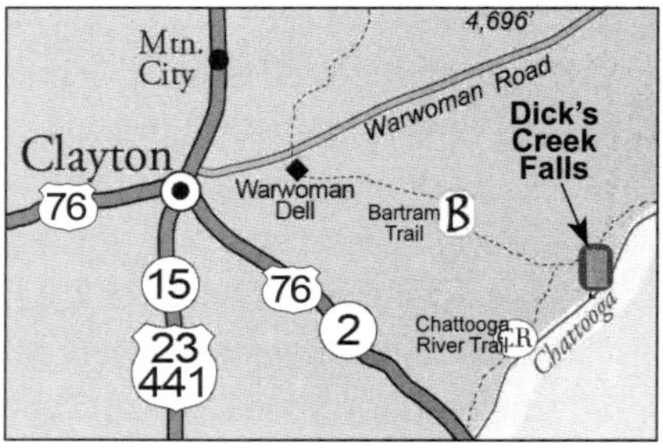

#36 Holcomb Creek Falls

Energetic hike featuring two wilderness waterfalls

Even with low water levels of late summer Holcomb Creek Falls is a beautiful place to visit.

Chattooga Ranger District
Chattahoochee National Forest
706.754.6221
GPS coordinates:
34.981745°N / 83.265357°W

- **2 scenic waterfalls**
- **0.5 mile (one way) to to 2.1 mile loop**
- **trout fishing closeby**

Wild and isolated, beautiful Holcomb Creek Falls actually features two waterfalls for the price of one. In addition to the 125' main cascade on Holcomb Creek, Ammons Creek Falls is a few hundred yards further up the same trail. From the trailhead descend moderately for 0.5 mile to a wooden footbridge spanning the creek below a boulder pile at the base of the cascade. The waterfall begins as several stair-stepping drops before chaotically racing across the rock face through a maze of boulders. Enjoy the view from the footbridge - the rocks around the waterfall are very slippery. Catch Holcomb Creek Falls at high water levels and it ranks up with the best in North Georgia. At lower levels not so much.

Continue along the trail and begin climbing moderately to Ammons Creek Falls just a few hundred yards ahead. A large wooden observation deck has been constructed just yards from this lively 40' cascade. A side path merges with the main trail just below Ammons and climbs back out to FS 7 about 0.6 mile west of the main trailhead creating a possible loop hike.

Directions: From Clayton take Warwoman Road (at the Days Inn) east for 9.7 miles to Hale Ridge Road (FS 7) on the left. Follow FS 7 for 6.6 miles to the intersection of FS 7 and Overflow Creek Road (FS 86). Park here. The trailhead is on the north side of the road (trail #52).

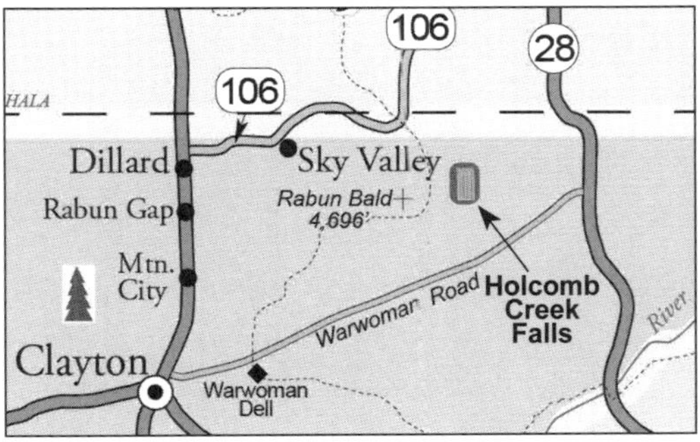

Mud Creek Falls #37

Beautiful roadside waterfall in Sky Valley

Sky Valley Resort
Tahoe Road
Sky Valley (near Dillard)
GPS coordinates:
34.986415°N / 83.330814°W

- **beautiful roadside cascade**

Mud Creek Falls may not sound too appealing on the surface but this easily viewed waterfall in Sky Valley is a surprisingly beautiful and powerful cascade. The waterfall is located just downstream of the Sky Valley golf course and visitors can drive right up to the base of this roaring 60' drop. Several "rooster tails" explode from the cliff face at higher water levels. The upper two-thirds of the waterfall plunges steeply while the lower third cascades rather gently over a series of shallow ledges. The falls are particularly inviting during the spring and summer months early in the morning as the forest greenery seems to envelope the falls in a soft green blanket. Be on your best behavior here and do not litter. We'd all love for Mud Creek Falls to be open to the general public for years to come.

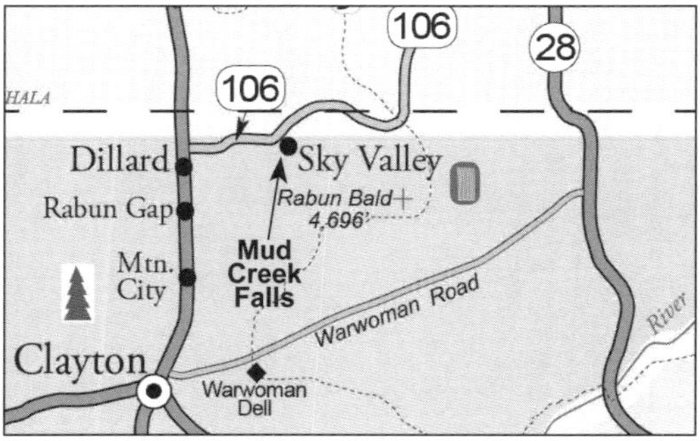

Directions: From U.S. 441 in Dillard take GA 246 north for 4.3 miles and turn right onto Bald Mountain Road. Proceed 0.9 mile and turn right into Sky Valley. Bear left then proceed 0.55 mile and turn right onto Tahoe Road. Dive 0.75 miles to the base of the falls.

#38 Bull Sluice

Thundering Class V rapid on the Chattooga River

Chattooga Wild & Scenic River
Chattooga Ranger District
Chattahoochee National Forest
706.754.6221
GPS coordinates:
34.8147°N / 83.3051°W

- **sandy beach on S.C. side**
- **swimming (caution!)**
- **picnicking**
- **whitewater boaters**

Bull Sluice - for another view look on page 126.

It's certainly not a "text book" waterfall in the classic sense but Bull Sluice *is* the very essence of falling water. This giant Class V rapid on the extraordinary Chattooga Wild & Scenic River has long been respected and even feared by members of the whitewater community. Unlike most Chattooga rapids it is easy to view - it is located a short walk from the USFS lot on the South Carolina side of the river. Some come to watch the boaters, some to wade or swim in the river, while some come just to catch some rays, but they do come. Visit here on a summer weekend and you certainly won't be alone.

The path from the parking area ends on the rocks high above the rapid. This is really the only safe place here. Most people do venture down toward the river but be aware that there have been *many* deaths at this spot. The rocks are very slippery, the current is surprisingly powerful and something about Bull Sluice seems to make people do really stupid things, like jumping from the top of the boulder pile on the Georgia side into the powerful chute below the rapid. Have fun taking in the scene but be very careful here. It's a popular spot to swim but there are risks. There is a wide sandy beach downriver by the highway bridge perfect for wading or for a nice relaxing picnic.

Directions: From Clayton take U.S. 76 east for 8.2 miles. Cross the Chattooga River and park in the large USFS Chattooga River parking lot on the left.

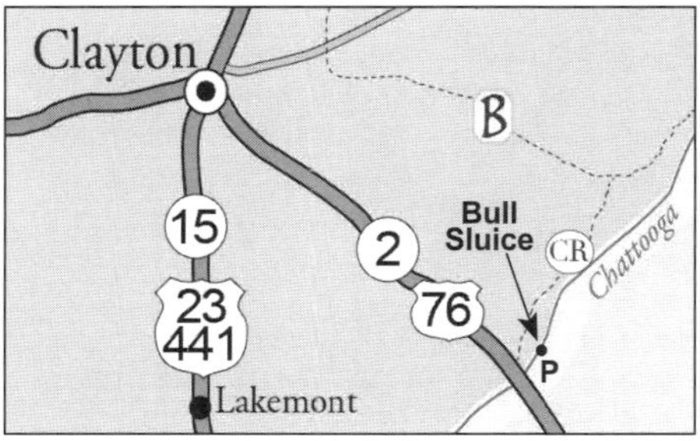

Waterfalls of Tallulah Gorge #39

Some of the Southeast's premier waterfalls reborn

Tallulah Gorge State Park
Tallulah Falls 30573
706.754-7981
www.gastateparks.org
GPS Coordinates:
34.739750°N / 083.395233°W

- **5 major falls**
- **4 falls can be viewed from easy rim trails**

We've already listed Tallulah Gorge State Park as a great North Georgia destination but the park's signature falls have to be included in this section spotlighting some of the state's best waterfalls. Luckily for most visitors four of the park's five major waterfalls can be seen from overlooks along the North and South Rim Trails. L'Eau d'or (45'), Tempesta (76'), Hurricane (96') *see photo above*, and Oceana (50') each have overlooks that focus on these mighty falls. Only Bridal Veil (aka Sliding Rock) demands visitors brave the rugged gorge floor hike (permit required). If you are hardy enough to tackle the 1,080 steps (total down and back) on the infamous stairway system you can get a close-up view of mighty Hurricane Falls from an observation deck perched high above this cascade's massive plunge pool.

For decades these falls were silent but a steady amount of water now flows through a culvert in the dam guaranteeing these beautiful wonders of nature will always flow. Visit during an aesthetic flow (check park schedule) and they'll be even better. Come during a whitewater release and see why Tallulah Falls was once known as the "Niagara of the South."

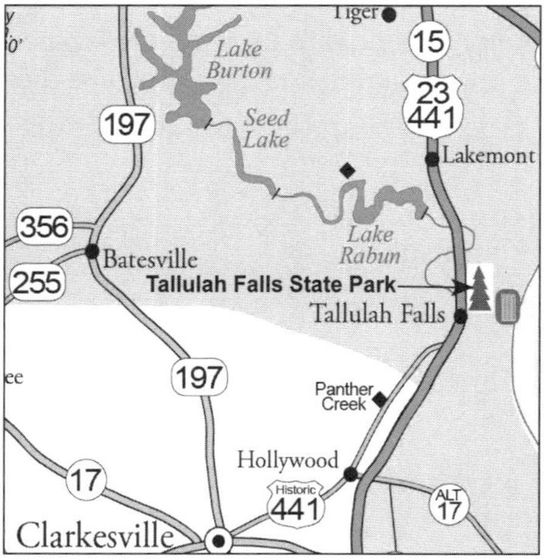

Directions: The park is located on U.S. 441 approximately 12 miles north of Clarkesville and 12 miles south of Clayton.

#40 Long Creek Falls

Pretty waterfall along the Appalachian Trail

Blue Ridge Ranger District
Chattahoochee National Forest
706.745.6928
GPS coordinates:
34.66833°N / 84.17305°W

- **1 mile (one way)**
- **moderate hike**
- **pretty 20' cascade**

One of the enticing things about Long Creek Falls is that the trip involves a walk on the legendary Appalachian Trail. In fact, the "side trail" that leads up to the waterfall is the very beginning of the Duncan Ridge Trail; it is also at the point where the Benton Mackaye Trail separates from the AT after sharing a common pathway. It sounds confusing but really all it takes is an easy-to-moderate one-mile (one way) walk from the Three Forks area on FS 58. At the one-mile point a marked side trail to the left leads about 100 yards up to the pretty cascade.

This part of the Appalachian Trail is only 6 miles north of the southern terminus at Springer Mountain and hiker traffic can be heavy during peak season in the early spring and on warm-weather weekends. The name Three Forks refers to the junction of Long, Chester and Stover Creeks. These three creeks merge to form colorfully named Noontootla Creek.

Directions: From Suches take GA 60 north for approximately 15.7 miles. Turn left onto Doublehead Gap Road and drive 5.7 miles and turn left onto FS 58. Follow FS 58 for approximately 5.5 miles to a series of roadside pull-offs at the Appalachian Trail crossing.

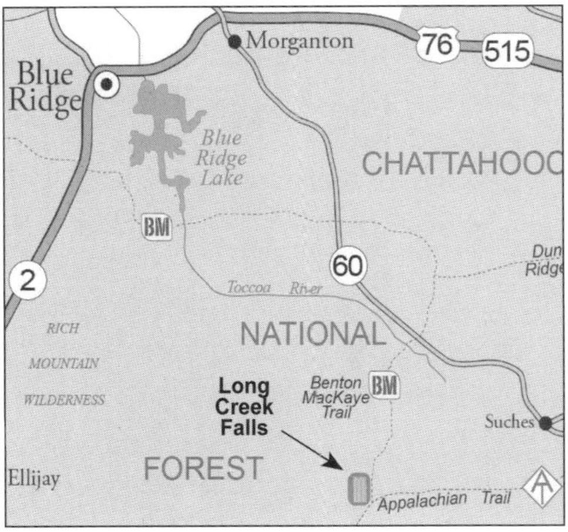

Jack's River Falls #41

One of the Cohutta Wilderness Area's most popular hikes

Cohutta Wilderness
Conasauga Ranger District
Chattahoochee National Forest
706.695.6736
GPS coordinates:
34.995556°N / 84.591111°W (parking area)
34.974722°N / 84.576944°W (base of falls)

- **4.5 miles (one way)**
- **large volume falls**
- **swimming hole upstream**

The rugged Cohutta Wilderness consists of nearly 37,000 acres of rugged mountain terrain featuring scores of miles of hiking trails and the headwaters of two pristine rivers - the Conasauga and Jack's. Spectacular Jack's River Falls is the most popular destination in the Cohuttas. The waterfall checks in at a respectable 50', but is quite powerful. In fact, more water flows over it than any other in North Georgia.

The most popular route is along the 4-mile Beech Bottom Trail which runs from the northern access parking area to the river. Once at the river turn right and follow the Jack's River Trail downstream for 0.5 mile to the top of the falls. A popular swimming hole is just upstream from the falls but be very cautious in your behavior as you are a long way from help. Accessing the base of the falls requires a steep slippery scramble as well. Because of the backcountry nature of this hike a detailed trail guide, maps or GPS equipment is advised. For those who are up to it, Jack's River Falls is a great destination.

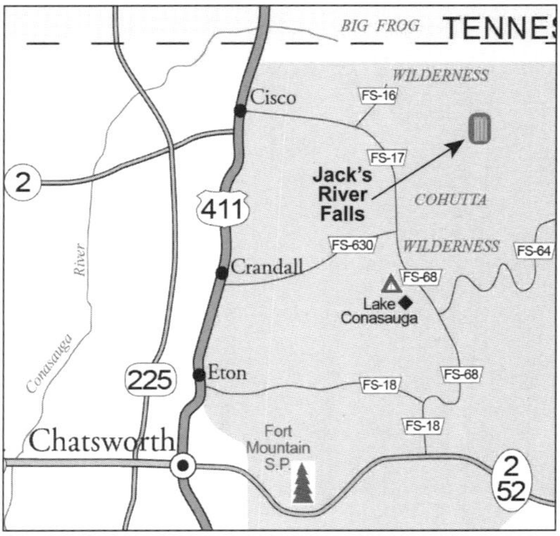

Directions: From Chatsworth take U.S. 411 north for 13 miles to Cisco. Turn right onto Old GA 2/FS 16 right before the Cisco Baptist Church. Proceed 10 miles (only the first 2 are paved) and turn right onto FS 62. Drive 4.4 miles to the Jack's River Trailhead.

#42 Falls of Cloudland Canyon

Thrilling hike to 2 classic free-falling waterfalls

Cloudland Canyon State Park
122 Cloudland Canyon Park Road
Rising Fawn, GA 30738
706.657.4050
www.gastateparks.org
GPS Coordinates:
34.8176°N / 85.4883°W

- **dramatic stairway descent into canyon**
- **moderate to strenuous "Waterfalls" Trail**

Waterfall #1, aka upper falls

Rugged Cloudland Canyon State Park was spotlighted briefly in Chapter 2, but the two beautiful waterfalls found deep in Sitton's Gulch deserve a special mention. A wonderfully executed stairway system, similar to the one at Tallulah Gorge State Park, descends into the Cloudland Canyon providing great views of the falls. Descriptively referred to as waterfall #1 and waterfall #2, or upper and lower falls, these classic free-falling waterfalls spill into deep plunge pools at the bases of imposing rock walls.

The Waterfalls Trail is about one mile total, but going all the way to the bottom for a view of lower falls requires around 1,200 steps round trip. Along the way hikers will pass dozens of fascinating and weird rock formations. If it reminds you of Rock City it's no wonder. You're basically on the same mountain. If you're not up to tackling the whole shebang the descent to view upper falls only, is much less strenuous, and in my opinion it is the prettier of the two (just my 2 cents) anyway. Hikers looking for more punishment can continue along the 6.5-mile Sitton's Gulch Loop Trail.

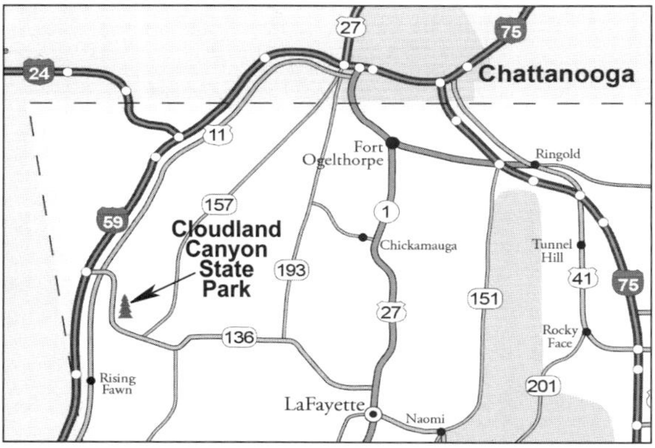

Directions: The park is located on GA 136 approximately 18 miles west of LaFayette and 8 miles east of Trenton; I-59 exit #11.

4
North Georgia's CLASSIC WALKS & HIKES

Brasstown Bald #43

Georgia's highest peak offers magnificent vistas

Blue Ridge Ranger District
Chattahoochee National Forest
www.fs.usda.gov
706.896.2556 or 706.745.6928
GPS Coordinates:
34.84789°N / 83.879856°W

Sunset from Brasstown Bald

- **scenic overlook**
- **picnicking**
- **hiking trails**
- **visitor center & exhibits**
- **Brasstown Wilderness Area**
- **closed in the Winter**
- **USFS fee area**

Georgia's highest peak soars to the majestic height of 4,784'. Engulfed within the rugged 12,600-acre Brasstown Wilderness, Brasstown Bald is easily accessible to visitors via dramatic 2.5-mile GA 180 spur which climbs several thousand feet to an enormous parking area about 0.5 mile (by foot) and several hundred vertical feet below the summit.

The unusual name "Brasstown" is said to have originated from a misunderstood translation. The Cherokee Indians who dwelt in the forests of North Georgia called the area *Itse'yi*, which means "new green place." Early settlers to the region supposedly mistook it for *Untsai'yi*, which means "brass." Whatever you call it this is a special mountain and each year tens of thousands of visitors make the trek to the cool, windblown summit.

From the parking area below the summit visitors may choose to reach the top either by riding in a concessionaire's van (for a nominal fee) or by walking the 0.5-mile paved trail. This path isn't overly steep but the grade never lets up during the ascent.

The U.S. Forest Service operates an expansive summit visitor center which features dozens of interesting exhibits on the history of the mountain and the natural environment of the Brasstown Bald area. Be sure to view the short video which is shown at regular intervals in the summit theater.

Museums and theaters are all well and good but the real reason everyone makes the drive up Brasstown Bald is to take in the 360° panorama from the observation deck atop the visitor center. This unusual circular viewing area offers unobstructed views of North Georgia and beyond. When conditions are favorable, views well into the mountains of North Carolina and Tennessee are visible.

The walk to the summit is very interesting as it traverses a forest of dwarf red and white oak, rosebay and purple rhododendron. The harsh conditions and relentless wind create a unique environment yet life flourishes on nearly every square inch of the mountain.

Be sure to dress for changing conditions. According to some sources the temperature has never exceeded the high 70s even in the sweltering heat of a North Georgia summer. Visitors often find that a day in the low 80s down low can turn into a chilly, windblown 60s on top of the mountain. Be prepared for the unexpected.

Hiking: Forget the car, you say. Let's walk up (or down) the mountain. Several hiking trails begin at the parking area and descend in various directions. The **Arkaquah Trail** descends west for 5.5 miles to Trackrock Gap on Trackrock Road. The 7-mile **Wagon Trail** descends in a northward direction to Young Harris College on U.S. 76 / Hwy. 2, and the **Jack's Knob Trail** runs south along a high ridge line to Jack's Gap on GA 180. The trail then climbs again to a junction with the Appalachian Trail at Chattahoochee Gap near the source of the Chattahoochee River.

Stargazing: Brasstown Bald features some of the darkest night skies in North Georgia and is a popular spot to stargaze. Whether you bring your own telescope or just want to lie on a blanket and enjoy the awe-inspiring night sky, Brasstown Bald offers a tremendous platform for enjoying creation at its very best.

Directions: From Helen take GA 75 north for approximately 12 miles and turn left onto GA 180. Proceed 6 miles and turn onto GA 180 spur. Follow the winding road 2.5 miles to the parking area.

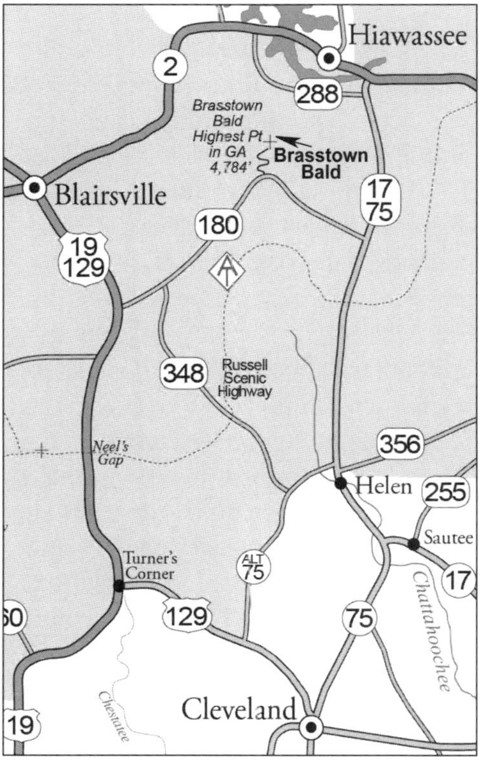

Blood Mountain #44

One of the Appalachian Trail's most popular day hikes

Blood Mountain Wilderness
Blue Ridge Ranger District
Chattahoochee National Forest
www.fs.usda.gov
706.745.6928
GPS Coordinates:
34.73959°N / 83.9370°W

Early morning atop Blood Mountain

- **4.4 to 6.5 miles**
- **classic Appalachain Trail day hike**
- **limit groups to 12 or less**
- **day hikers must use Reese Spur Trail**

The rugged summit of lofty Blood Mountain (4,458') has been a favorite North Georgia day hiker destination for generations - and for good reason. The Appalachian Trail crosses busy U.S. 19/129 at Neel's Gap, the home of Mountain Crossings at Walasi-yi, a popular hiking outfitter and thru-hiker resource. Blood Mountain is the first major summit the Georgia portion of the AT crosses, and since the 2.2 mile (one way) trek is within an average hiker's reach it has become a very popular destination.

Legend has it that Blood Mountain attained its name due to an unusually bloody conflict between native tribes perhaps centuries ago, but the only battle taking place here today is the one you'll wage with your own legs and lungs as you tackle the relentless path to the summit.

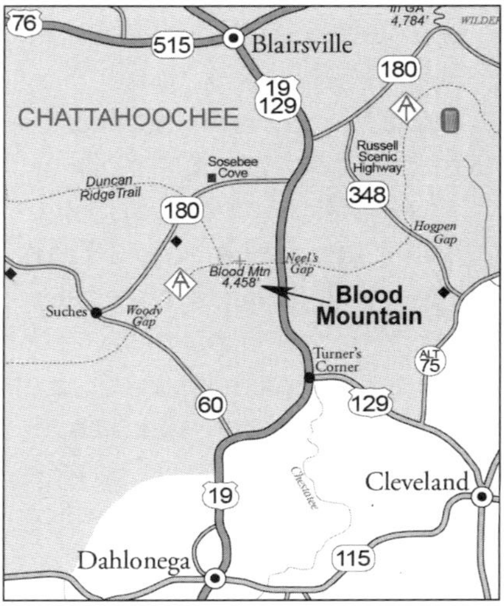

Though Neel's Gap offers the most direct access to the summit day hikers are required to continue north along the highway for 0.3 mile and park in the Reece Memorial day hiker parking area. The elevation here is about 3,000'. A 0.4-mile spur trail climbs steeply up to Flatrock Gap (elevation 3,460') and the AT. The distance from Flatrock Gap to the summit is an additional 1.5 miles. Oh, and by the way, you'll climb another 1,000 vertical feet as well.

Blood Mountain's has a unusually open summit with a number of rock outcrops that offer long range views. A heavily-utilized hiking shelter built by the Civilian Conservation Corps in the 1930s offers overnight visitors solid shelter from the elements. If you plan on using the shelter you'd better plan on sharing it with other hikers.

Blood Mountain's rugged summit is particularly alluring in the late spring and early summer when laurel, rhododendron and seasonal wildflowers compete for your attention.

Alternate trails: There are a number of great trails that tie into the Appalachian Trail in the Blood Mountain vicinity providing day hikers with several options. One of the most popular day hikes involves the 1.8-mile **Freeman Trail** which shortcuts the Blood Mountain summit. It begins at Bird Gap on the west and winds along the southern flank of Blood Mountain before rejoining the AT at Flatrock Gap on the east.

Other trails that you may consider for a scenic day hike would be the **Slaughter Gap Trail** (2.7 miles) and the **Jarrard Gap Trail** (1.2 miles) which climb from nearby Lake Winfield Scott Recreation Area on GA 180 up to the Appalachian Trail west of Blood Mountain. If you'd prefer to stay solely on the Appalachian Trail it is a beautiful 11.5 mile hike from Neel's Gap southwest to Woody Gap.

When to go: Don't ever forget that this is one of the busiest sections of the Appalachian Trail in Georgia. On choice warm weather weekends the parking areas, trail and summit can become quite crowded. Plan your trip accordingly. If you're an early riser your chances of solitude are much better.

Don't forget to hydrate: Use plenty of common sense on any summit hike, even when it's only 4-6 miles round trip. Bring plenty of drinking water. While there are several springs along the trail don't depend on water sources being available. This is a demanding hike and you're sure to work up a good sweat.

Directions: Neel's Gap is located on U.S. 19/129 approximately 18 miles north of Cleveland, 21 miles north of Dahlonega and approximately 10 miles south of Blairsville.

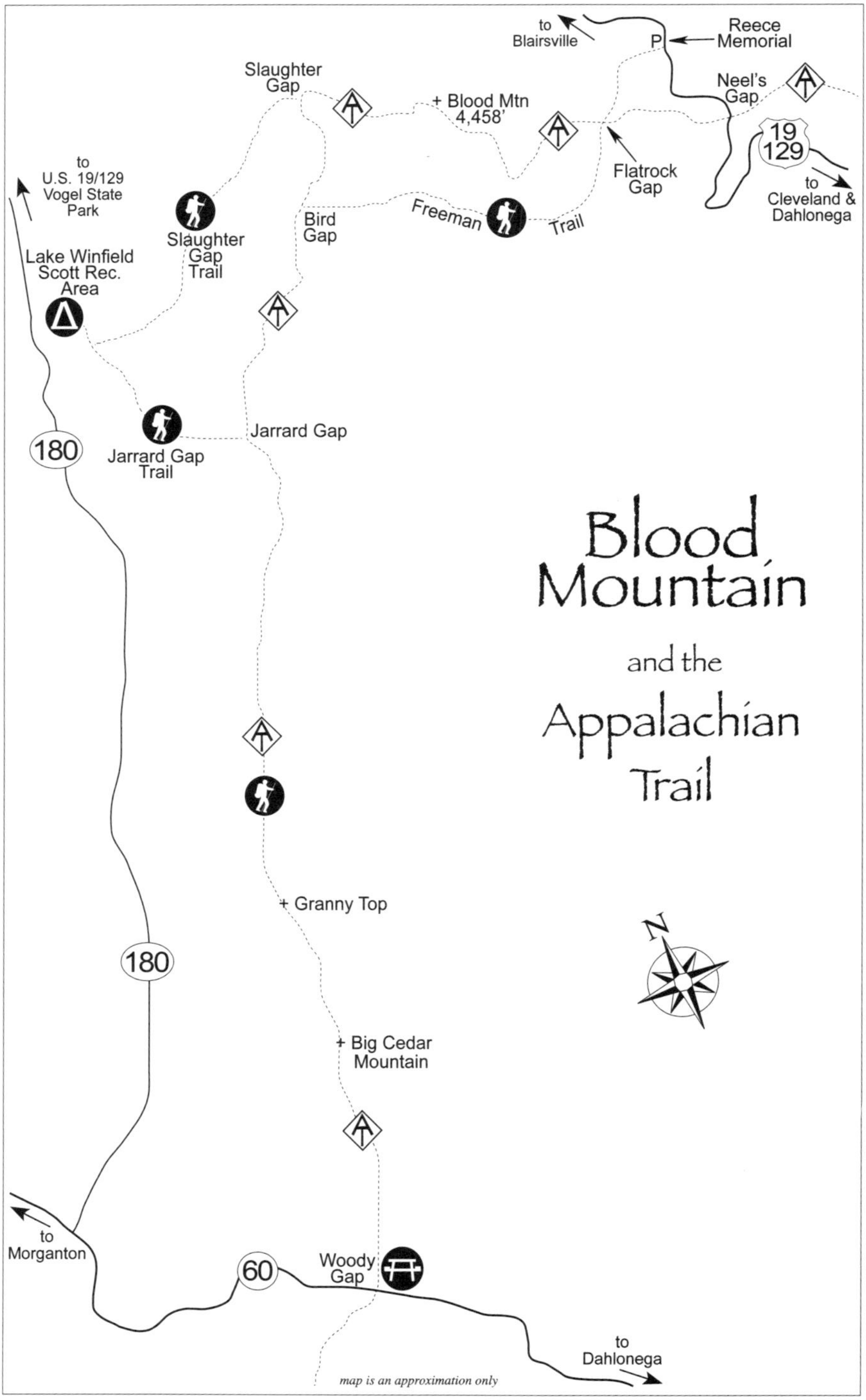
to
Blairsville
P
Reece
Memorial
Slaughter
Gap
+ Blood Mtn
4,458'
Neel's
Gap
19
129
to
U.S. 19/129
Vogel State
Park
Flatrock
Gap
to
Cleveland &
Dahlonega
Slaughter
Gap
Trail
Bird
Gap
Freeman Trail
Lake Winfield
Scott Rec.
Area
Jarrard Gap
180
Jarrard Gap
Trail
Blood
Mountain
and the
Appalachian
Trail
+ Granny Top
N
180
+ Big Cedar
Mountain
to
Morganton
60
Woody
Gap
to
Dahlonega
map is an approximation only

#45 Big Cedar Mountain

Short stroll on the AT offers a big view

Appalachian Trail
Blue Ridge Ranger District
Chattahoochee National Forest
Phone: 706.754.6928
GPS coordinates:
34.6890°N / 83.9922°W

- **scenic vistas**
- **great day hike**
- **1.25 miles (one way)**
- **picnic tables at Woody Gap**

From the AT just below the Big Cedar summit

Coming in at 3,721', Big Cedar Mountain is officially Georgia's 41st highest peak. Obviously it isn't one of the state's major mountains but it does offer an outstanding easterly vista from three rocky overlooks near the summit. The walk from Woody Gap is easy to moderate with a climb of less than 600 vertical feet. The first 0.7 mile is really little more than a leisurely stroll through an open hardwood forest. The final 0.5-mile segment requires a bit more effort as the trail switchbacks up the southern flank of Big Cedar (which ironically seems surprisingly lacking in cedars).

All three overlooks are just off the main trail along prominent side paths. One is actually very close to the actual summit but it is probably the least desirable of the three. One has even garnered its own nickname, "Preacher's Rock." The overlooks are on the eastern side of Big Cedar Mountain offering views to the east and south. In the "foreground" to the south is the Waters Creek watershed.

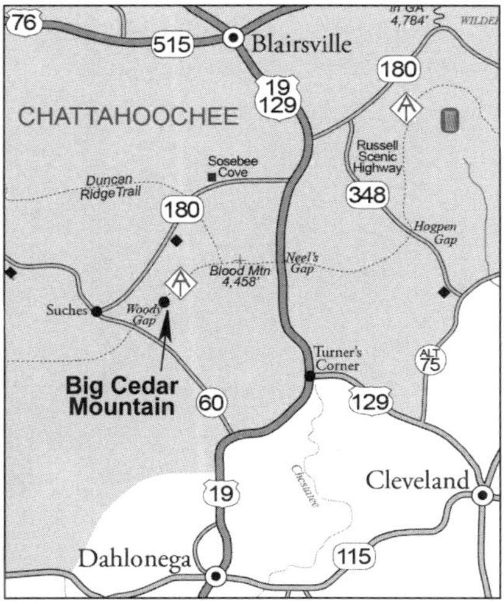

Directions: Woody Gap is located along GA 60 approximately 14 miles north of Dahlonega, about 3 miles south of Suches, and 29 miles south of Morganton.

Tray Mountain #46

Georgia's "other" AT summit offers magnificent views

Tray Mountain Wilderness
Chattooga Ranger District
Chattahoochee National Forest
706.747.3816
GPS coordinates:
34.801205°N / 83.683785°W

- **scenic vistas**
- **classic AT day hike**
- **botanically rich area**
- **one mile (one way)**

Tray Mountain is the eighth highest peak in Georgia (4,430') and is perhaps second in popularity among AT day hikes in the state behind Blood Mountain. The shortest route to Tray Mountain's tiny open summit is within reach of nearly anyone in reasonably good physical condition. From the intersection of FS 698 and FS 79 it's just a little less than one mile to the summit. Couch potatoes, don't get too excited - it takes a 600' climb to reach the top - a few hundred feet less than climbing, say, Stone Mountain in Atlanta.

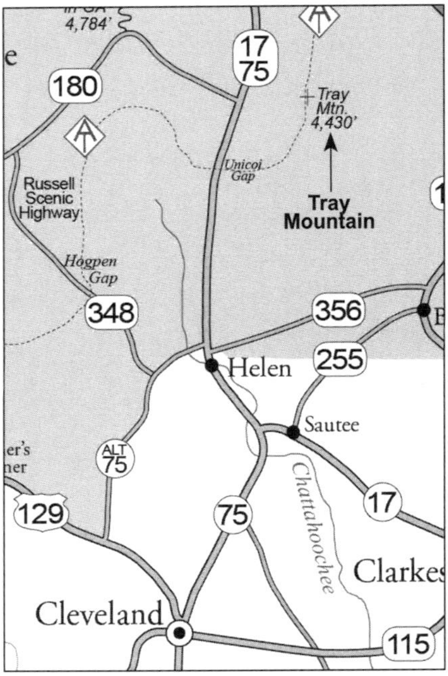

Most of the route follows a series of broad, looping switchbacks which allows you to enjoy the surrounding forest without constantly struggling to catch your breath. At least one limited overlook is encountered along the way but it is just a tease for the big view on top.

The actual summit of Tray Mountain is surprisingly small, especially compared to Blood Mountain's broad expanse of exposed rock which allows hikers to spread out. The scenery is exceptional. The surrounding peaks of the Chattahoochee National Forest and North Georgia rise dramatically before you. To the

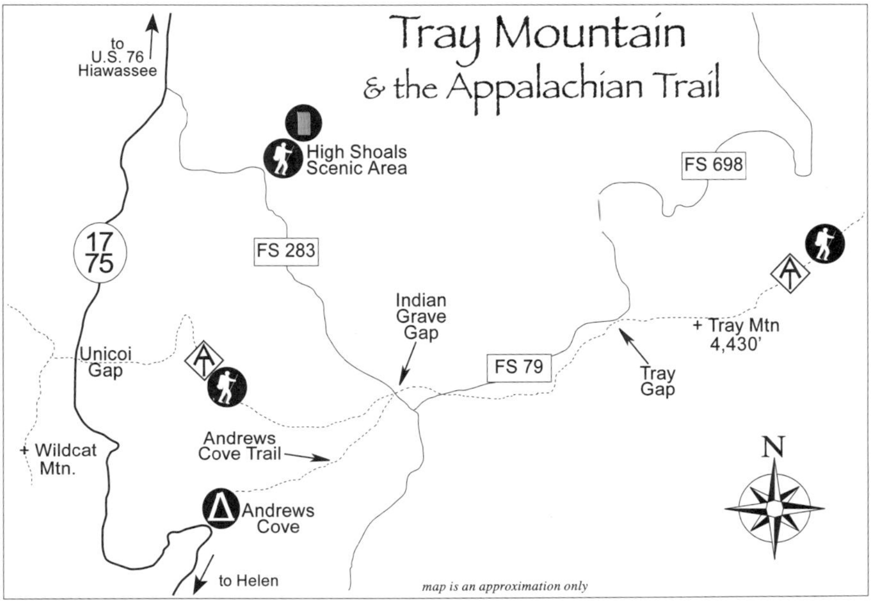

south the unmistakable profile of Cleveland's Mt. Yonah, the highest point in the Georgia piedmont, rises prominently from the rolling hills of White County. Look to the east and several narrow arms of beautiful Lake Burton are visible. On exceptionally clear days, even the unmistakable profile of the aforementioned Stone Mountain in Atlanta is visible.

Tray doesn't normally attract the same type of crowds as Blood Mountain but it still becomes quite congested on weekends and in the summer months. If you find the summit crowded during your visit, try walking an additional several hundred yards north along the AT. Look for a side trail that branches to the right out to a southern-facing overlook.

Alternate hikes: This portion of the Appalachian Trail stretches 16.1 miles from Unicoi Gap along GA 17/75 to Dick's Creek Gap on U.S. 76 between Hiawassee and Clayton. This makes a great long day hike or, even better yet, an overnighter. Another day hike option is to work in the 2-mile Andrews Cove Trail into your hike. Keep in mind that it's all uphill from Andrews Cove to the AT.

Directions: From Helen take GA 75 north for 11 miles. Turn right onto FS 283 (2 miles north of Unicoi Gap). This is the road for High Shoals Scenic Area. Drive 4 miles then turn sharply left (east) onto FS 79. Drive 2 miles to the junction with FS 698 and the Appalachian Trail.

Wildcat Mountain #47

Short AT spur trail leads to peaceful summit vistas

Raven Cliffs Wilderness
Chattooga Ranger District
Chattahoochee National Forest
706.747.3816
GPS coordinates:
34.71926°N / 83.83935°W

- **0.7 mile (one way)**
- **scenic views**
- **nice wilderness picnic spot**
- **interesting terrain**

Looking north from the Wildcat summit

Unicoi Gap is a well-known Appalachian Trail gateway, but a lesser-known trail just a short walk away breaks south from the AT near Unicoi Gap and takes hikers to the elongated summit of 2,780' Wildcat Mountain. AT hikers are familiar with this spur trail as the route to the Whitley Gap Shelter. Day hikers familiar with the area know that Wildcat features several open rock outcrops offering big views.

Follow the AT south along a series of steep switchbacks from Hogpen Gap to the Whitley Gap Spur Trail. Turn left onto the spur and climb easily toward the summit. This portion of the trail traverses a beautiful ridgeline covered with mossy rocks tucked beneath thick stands of laurel. Locate the prominent side paths on the summit which drop to the right to an open expanse of granite offering long range views. Whether you're hiking the AT or just out sightseeing, the short stroll to Wildcat Mountain might be well worth the effort.

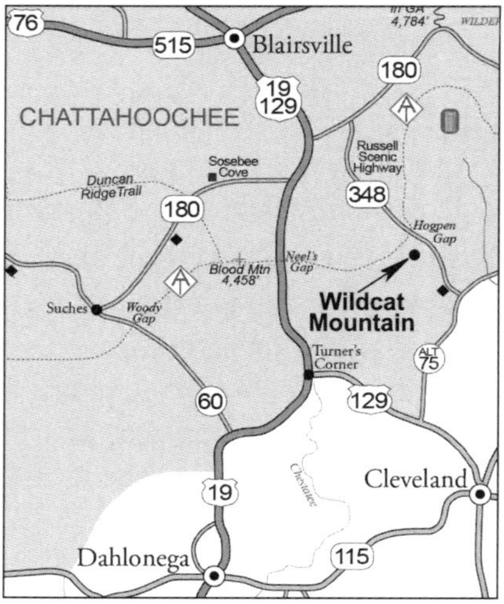

Directions: From Helen drive north on GA 17/75 for 1.5 miles. Turn left onto GA 75 ALT and drive 2.3 miles to GA 348 (Russell Scenic Hwy.) on the right. Take GA 348 for approximately 7 miles to Hogpen Gap and park. Cross the highway and take the AT south up to the Whitley Gap Spur Trail.

#48 Sosebee Cove

Short hike features rare plants and geology

Dwarf crested iris

Sosebee Cove Scenic Area
Blue Ridge Ranger District
Chattahoochee National Forest
Phone: 706.754.6928
GPS coordinates:
34.78509°N / 83.93324°W

- **0.3 mile loop trail**
- **botanically rich area**

Beautiful Sosebee Cove is a cool, shady north-facing cove situated at an average elevation of 2,200'. The cove features a wonderful variety of unique flora and fauna more commonly found in forests much farther north. Trees found here include tulip poplar, buckeyes, maples and basswood. A fascinating boulder field that is somewhat common on north-facing coves is visible along the highway. Wildflowers are common in the warmer months and in late spring and early summer there is a tremendous variety of blooming color in the cove.

The short but scenic 0.3-mile loop trail winds through the cove in the shape of a figure-8. The trail crosses tiny Wolf Creek several times as it descends into the forest. This 175-acre area is preserved as a living memorial to Arthur Woody, affectionately known as the "barefoot ranger." Ranger Woody served with the U.S. Forest Service from 1918 to 1945 and was instrumental in purchasing the cove by the Forest Service. Some knowledgeable sources consider Sosebee Cove to be the best second-growth stand of yellow poplar in the country.

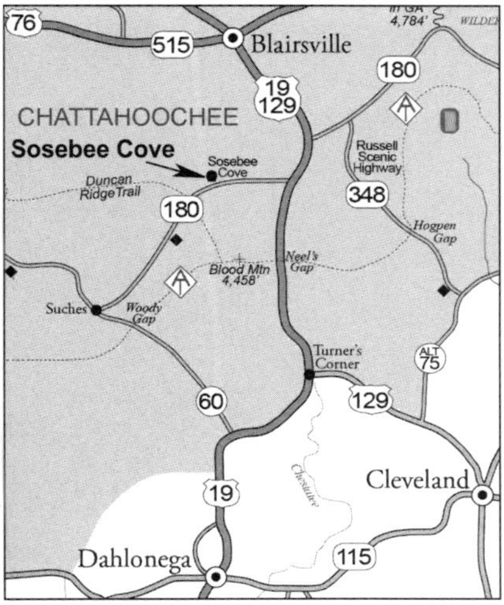

Directions: From Blairsville take U.S. 19/129 south for 10 miles. Turn right onto GA 180 (just prior to Vogel State Park) and drive 2 miles to the paved pull-off on the right.

Raven Cliffs #49

Popular day hike offers waterfalls, cliffs and more

Raven Cliffs Wilderness
Chattooga Ranger District
Chattahoochee National Forest
706.754.6221
GPS coordinates:
34.718704°N / 83.80907°W

- **beautiful 2.5 mile (one way) day hike**
- **unusual rock formation and hidden waterfall**
- **follows scenic Dodd Creek the entire way**

Raven Cliffs Falls hides deep within a rocky recess.

The beautiful 9,649-acre Raven Cliffs Wilderness is home to several outstanding trails. Several miles of the famous Appalachian Trail passes through the northern flank of this protected wilderness within the Chattahoochee National Forest. One of North Georgia's most popular trails is found here as well - the delightful Raven Cliffs Trail.

This blue-blazed path originates at a parking area just off the Richard Russell Scenic Highway (GA 348). It closely follows splashing Dodd Creek upstream and features three small waterfalls en route before ending at Raven Cliffs at mile 2.5. The small waterfalls include a 12' drop at mile 1.0, and an impressive 25' drop about 1.5 miles from the trailhead.

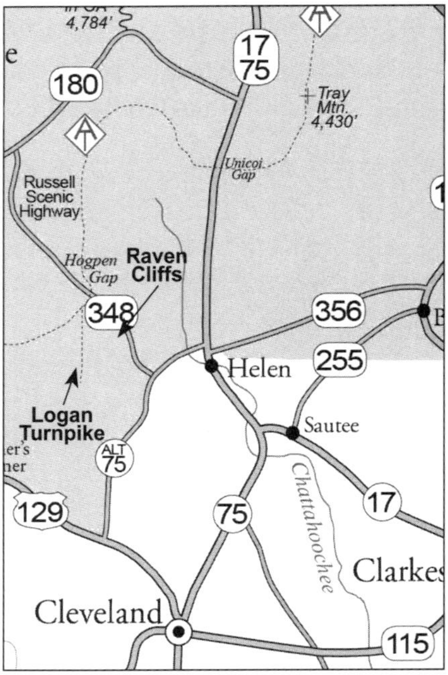

The trail gains a little over 850' feet in its 2.5-mile journey to the cliffs though the gain is so gradual it feels much less. In other words you'll get a great workout without even knowing it.

The trail ends dramatically at the foot of an enormous grey wall of rock known as Raven Cliffs. As you approach it appears that Dodd Creek vanishes into the cliff. A vertical cleft in the rock soon comes into view and Raven Cliffs can be seen free-falling within a dark recess. Without a doubt, it's one of the most unique waterfalls in Georgia.

Work your way uphill along the prominent social trail and you'll come face-to-face with another very unusual Raven Cliffs feature. When the path runs out a primitive path known as the "root ladder" allows the truly adventurous up to the top of the cliffs where another cascade plunges upstream, behind the cliffs. This climb to the top of the cliffs is not without risk but hundreds of people do it every warm-weather weekend. If you do not use extreme caution this is a location where a tragedy could easily occur. If you are afraid of heights, forget the cliff tops. It's a great spot to watch people rappel down the sheer cliffs (from the bottom, of course).

When to go: This is definitely one of North Georgia's most popular day-hike destinations. Do not come here on a sunny warm weekend and expect to find solitude. You may well find dozens *if not hundreds* of fellow hikers.

Directions: From Helen drive north on GA 17/75 for 1.5 miles. Turn left onto GA 75 ALT and drive 2.3 miles to GA 348 (Russell Scenic Hwy) on the right. Drive 2.9 miles to the Raven Cliffs parking area on the left.

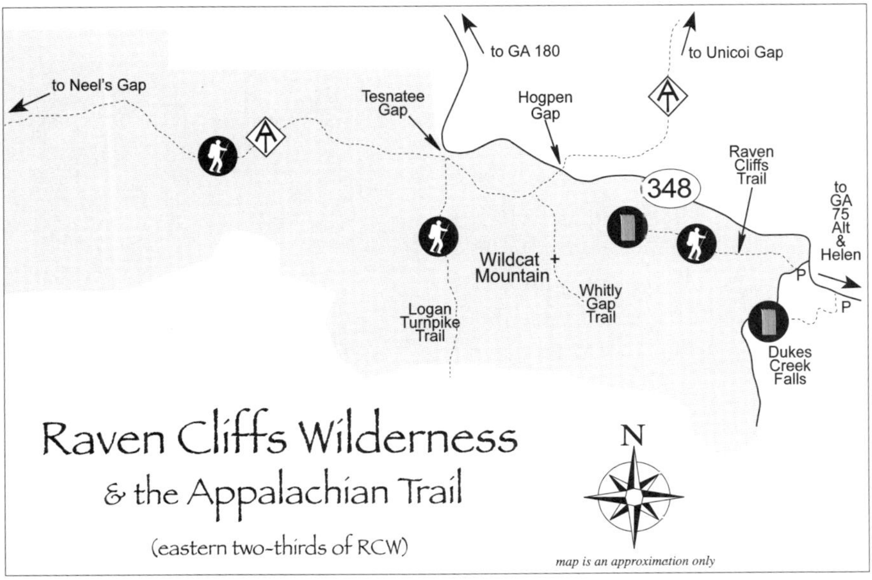

Sliding Rock Trail #50

Spectacular hike to Georgia's most dramatic swimming hole

Tallulah Gorge State Park - Rabun County
338 Jane Hurt Yarn Drive
Tallulah Falls, GA 30573
706.754-7981
www.gastateparks.org
GPS Coordinates:
34.739750°N / 083.395233°W

- **difficult 1 mile trail**
- **incomparable Sliding Rock**
- **900' elevation change**
- **dangerous gorge floor**

Tallulah Gorge State Park has some great hiking trails, but nothing comes close to the thrill of hiking along the floor of this rugged gorge and witnessing the dramatic landscape from river-level. For 100 lucky (early) hikers who are able to secure permits each day it is a boulder-scrambling, rock-hopping one mile adventure to everyone's favorite summertime destination - Sliding Rock.

Sliding Rock (aka Bridal Veil Falls) is as far as one can venture downstream in the gorge. The main route involves descending over 530 stairs to the base of Hurricane Falls, then rock-hopping across the river and working your way down to Sliding Rock. It's tricky and takes a lot of time and effort but those who persevere are rewarded with 3 beautiful waterfalls and magnificent swimming hole set against towering cliffs reaching hundreds of feet into the air. The real payoff is the thrilling ride down the waterfall into the massive plunge pool. Be careful - it's really slippery, but there's nothing else quite like it in North Georgia. Get your permit early!

Directions: Tallulah Gorge State Park is located approximately half way between Clarkesville and Clayton on U.S. 441.

#51 Coleman River Trail

Old growth timber and splashing cascades

Enjoying a Coleman cascade

Coleman River Scenic Area
Chattooga Ranger District
Chattahoochee National Forest
706.754.6221
GPS coordinates:
34.92981°N / 83.54571°W

- **one mile (one way)**
- **scenic stream**
- **close proximity to Rock Gorge and Tate City**
- **camping nearby**
- **trout fishing**

Coleman River is actually more like Coleman Creek, but what this stream lacks in size it more than makes up for in spirit. A popular one-mile (one way) trail makes its way upstream alongside tumbling Coleman River past dozens of small shoals, lively cascades and some massive streamside boulders and rock slabs. Beginning at an elevation just a few feet under 2,000', the pathway is relatively mild overall but a few moderate grades get your heart pumping just a bit.

The Coleman River valley is quite narrow and fairly steep but a few areas along the path are flat enough for a streamside picnic. The trail abruptly ends about one mile above the bridge at the edge of the rugged Southern Nantahala Wilderness.

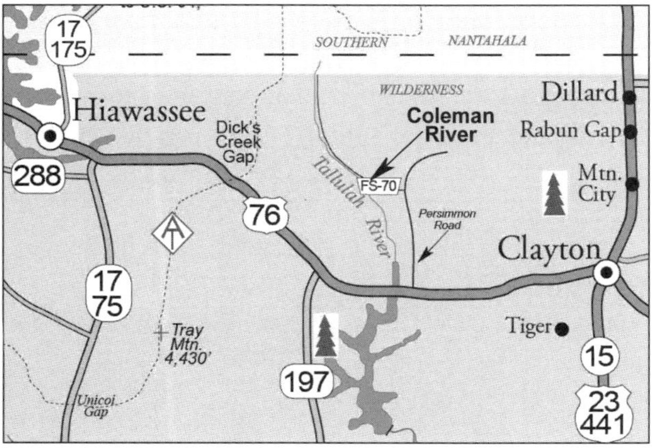

Directions: Starting in Clayton take U.S. 76 west for 8 miles. Turn right onto Persimmon Road and drive north for 4 miles. Turn left onto Tallulah River Road (FS 70) and drive 1.2 miles to the Coleman River bridge and trailhead.

Rabun Bald #52

Spectacular panorama from Georgia's second highest peak

Chattooga Ranger District
Chattahoochee National Forest
706.754.6221
GPS coordinates:
34.965561°N / 83.300003°W
34.979167°N / 83.303056°W (Bee Gum Gap)

- **0.5 mile (one way) to 1.5 miles (one way)**
- **spectacular long range vistas**
- **approximate 1,000' elevation change**

Massive Rabun Bald stands as a sentinel along Georgia's northeastern corner. Checking in at a lofty 4,696', Rabun Bald is the state's second highest peak, about 88' shorter than Brasstown Bald. While the two peaks are similar in height, Rabun Bald offers a distinctively different summit experience from the development and crowds atop Brasstown Bald. The total lack of facilities and the somewhat challenging trailhead make Rabun Bald one of Georgia's wildest locations.

There are several routes to the summit but for purposes of this guide we will deal with the shortest route. A spur trail leads from Bee Gum Gap (where parking is very limited) over to the Bartram Trail creating a 1.5-mile summit trek (one way) that gains around 1,000 vertical feet. The easier and more popular route is to drive up the rocky, bumpy gravel road to a small parking area below the summit. Believe me, this road is unsuitable for passenger vehicles. The Bartram Trail intersects this upper parking lot before continuing its climb to the summit, only a short 0.5-mile hike away.

This last half-mile climbs through a series of moderately steep switchbacks as it tunnels through a dense grove of mountain laurel and rhododendron. As it climbs higher onto the summit ridge line it flattens somewhat before emerging into the open bald atop the summit.

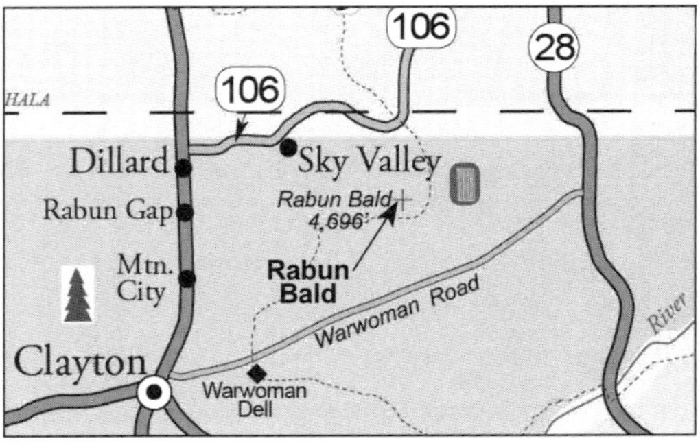

One of the first fire towers in Georgia was constructed at the summit and remained in operation until the 1970s. A wooden observation deck was constructed atop the

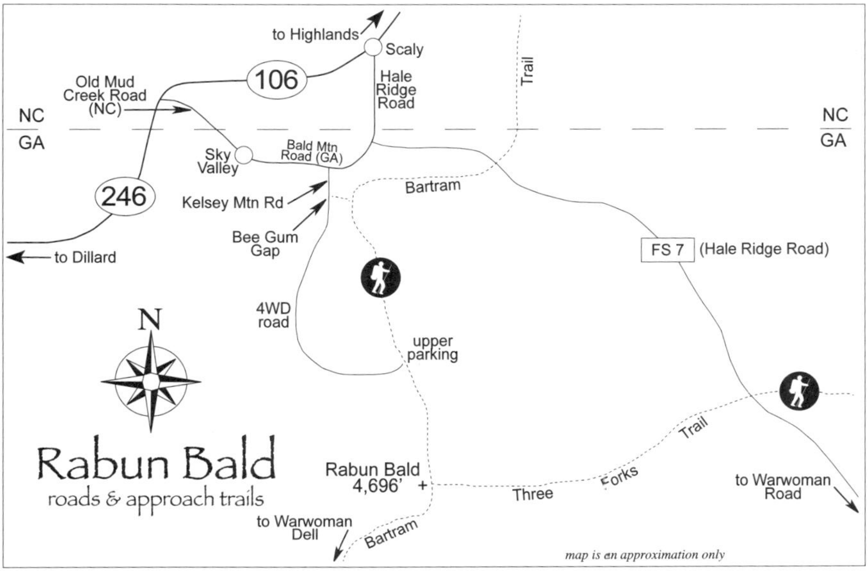

tower's stacked rock base reaching about 20' off the ground. Visitors who make the trek are treated to one of the best long-range views in North Georgia. Views of 80-90 miles are possible, well into North Carolina's Nantahala Mountains and east into the South Carolina piedmont.

Several optional routes are available at the summit. The steep **Three Forks Trail** drops from the summit to Hale Ridge Road (FS 7) about 3 miles distant. It then continues another 6 miles to the West Fork Chattooga River. The renowned **Bartram Trail** stretches south from the summit 17.5 miles to Warwoman Dell just east of Clayton.

Directions: From Dillard and U.S. 441 turn east onto GA 246 and proceed 4.3 miles to the Sinclair store on the right. Turn right here onto Old Mud Creek Road (which becomes Bald Mountain Road when it crosses back into Georgia before reaching Sky Valley). Drive 2.8 miles to Kelsey Mountain Road (look for the USFS sign for Rabun Bald). Drive 0.3 mile to Bee Gum Gap.

Park here, well off the road, making sure you don't park on anyone's property (don't block any driveways!) Here the 4WD road branches right and heads to the upper parking area about 1.1 miles up the mountain. To the left of the gap about 100 yards into the woods, a side path connects with the Bartram Trail. Turn right, then ascend to the upper parking lot, and ultimately, the summit, by this route.

Yonah Mountain #53

Heart-pumping walk to the highest point in the Georgia piedmont

Chattooga Ranger District
Chattahoochee National Forest
706.754.6221
GPS coordinates:
34.637429°N / 83.772577°W (parking lot)
34.639214°N / 83.714806°W (summit)

- **strenuous 2.4 miles (one way)**
- **sheer cliffs**
- **fantastic views**
- **primitive camping area**

Though enticingly close to the mountains of North Georgia, Yonah Mountain is actually a part of the Georgia piedmont region. In fact, it is officially the highest point in Georgia's piedmont - 3,166'. The mountain's distinctive profile and sheer rock walls make it a popular rock climbing and rappelling destination (the U.S. Army Rangers actually train here). In 2007, a challenging trail was opened that runs from the base of the mountain to the top. The trail is about 2.4 miles (one way) and gains approximately 1,400 feet, enough to put it in the strenuous category.

From the lower parking area the trail loops along the southeastern slopes of the mountain through a mixed hardwood forest. The climb is steady but not too bad. Around the one-mile point the trail emerges into a scenic west-facing clearing before climbing *steeply* to a point roughly half way up the mountain (known as the "staging area" to rock climbers). You'll find several privies here. From here on to the summit a number of paths lead out to popular climbing routes. The summit views are excellent, but be on guard for deadly drop-offs. Also, keep a sharp eye on the weather. This is one place you do not want to be in a thunderstorm! I know this from personal experience.

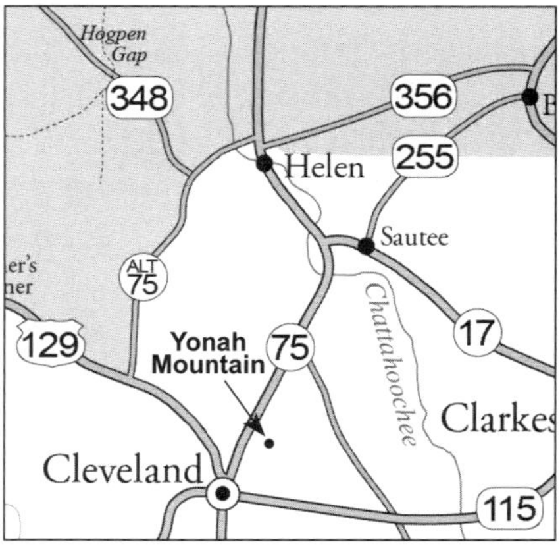

Directions: From Cleveland take GA 75 north for about 3 miles. Turn right onto Tom Bell Road (at the Western Sizzlin'). Make a quick left onto Chambers Road, then look for the second gravel road on the left which leads to the parking area.

#54 James Edmonds Backcountry Trail

One of the Georgia state park system's most challenging trails

Lookoff Mountain Overlook

Black Rock Mountain State Park
3085 Black Rock Mountain Parkway
Mountain City, GA 30562
706.746.2141
www.gastateparks.org
GPS Coordinates:
34.907201°N / 083.412062°W (trailhead)

- **7.2 mile loop**
- **equivalent of 2,400' elevation change**
- **scenic views**
- **backcountry camping**

Black Rock Mountain State Park's most challenging trail was named in honor of one of its first rangers. This 7.2-mile trail features a series of ascents and descents that are the equivalent of about 2,000 vertical feet! It's a tough trail but the rewards are worth the effort. Average walk time for fit individuals - about 4 hours. The Edmonds Backcountry Trail (JEBT) and Tennessee Rock Trails share the same trailhead, so be sure to follow the signs and use the free park map which you can get at the summit visitor center.

The JEBT features very little flat ground so do *not* underestimate it. *Switchback* was not a word prominently in the minds of the designers so be in good shape or choose another trail. Hikers are encouraged to hike this trail in a clockwise direction. After the initial 0.7 mile the trail comes to a fork. For purposes of this guide we're turning right at the fork.

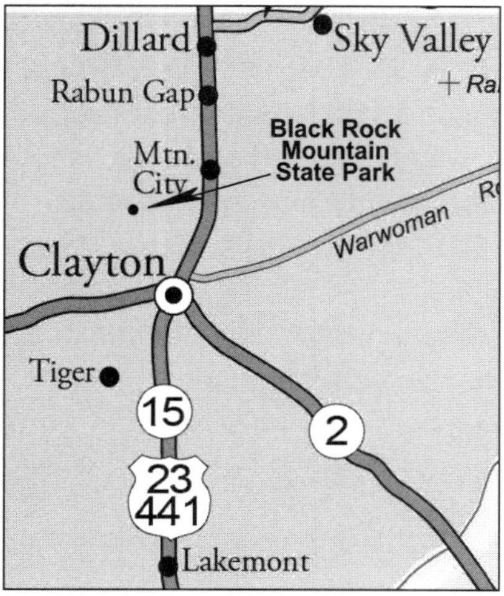

In general the initial 2.5 miles descend from around 3,300' elevation at the trailhead across North Germany Road to approximately 2,400' at the Taylor Creek crossing. Black Rock's northeastern slopes are generally cool and shady and a wide variety of wildflowers bloom throughout the spring and summer.

If you really love hills, the fun starts here as the next obstacle is a heart-pounding 600' ascent of Scruggs

Knob (elevation 3,048') through an impressive grove of gnarled and twisted mountain laurel. At mile 3.5 you have a choice - the spur trail to the right climbs 0.7 mile to the rocky summit of Lookoff Mountain (3,162'). Two backcountry campsites are located in this area (permit required). The overlooks along the spur trail are absolutely fantastic offering spectacular views of Wolffork Valley and the Dillard area. The overlooks are perched atop sheer granite cliffs and are perfect sites for a hard-earned picnic.

Backtrack to the main JEBT loop and turn right to continue. Over the next mile make a moderate descent and intersect Taylors Chapel Road at mile 4.5. This crossing occurs at beautiful 17-acre Black Rock Lake at an elevation of 2,241'.

If you've barely worked up a sweat, you may want to complete the easy 0.85-mile loop trail around the lake. It features several nice boardwalks and plenty of scenery. You might even want to wet a line and catch a few fish.

If you are feeling a bit tired at this point you might want to lie down and ready yourself for the next leg of the hike. When you're ready, get back on the JEBT and follow the trail along the southern shoreline of Black Rock Lake past the Creek Ridge Backcountry Campsite #4.

The trail then crosses the wonderfully named Greasy Creek upstream through lush stands of native rhododendron. The grade is fairly steep but the relative lack of switchbacks makes it seem somewhat worse than it really is. A second crossing over the creek signals an intersection with North Germany Road near the park's main gate.

Beyond this crossing you've entered the "home stretch." The trail negotiates yet another fairly steep slope as it switchbacks up to the original fork. Climb several hundred vertical feet along the original 0.7 mile section back to the trailhead. Congratulations - you've just burned 1,000 calories or more and unlike most of the park's visitors, you've seen the sights the old fashioned way - on foot.

Directions: From Clayton take U.S. 441 north into Mountain City. Turn left onto Black Rock Mountain Parkway and proceed up the mountain into the park. The trailhead is located on Black Rock Mountain Parkway approximately half way between the campground turnoff and the summit visitor center.

• *Reference Black Rock Mountain State Park map on page 29.*

#55 Keown Falls Scenic Area

Scenic hike to the disappearing waterfall with the big view

Falling water from Keown Falls streaks against a sunlit backdrop

Keown Falls Scenic Area
Conasauga Ranger District
706.695.6736
GPS Coordinates:
34.613898°N / 085.08599°W

- **1.8 mile loop**
- **moderate to strenuous**
- **check creek flow to see if falls is flowing**
- **excellent overlook**

You'll probably come for the waterfall, but what you will remember is the long range scenic vista. Keown Falls free-falls about 50' high atop the eastern flank of John's Mountain. It's a popular sight, but the stream flow is quite small. Much of the year it doesn't amount to more than a trickle, and it usually dries up entirely in the summer and fall. The waterfall is named for Gordon Keown who was an alumnus of Berry College in Rome and surveyed much of northwest Georgia.

The 218-acre Keown Falls Scenic Area features a 1.8-mile loop trail that climbs the mountain up to the waterfall. The trailhead recreation area features picnic tables and a restroom. From the recreation area follow the trail into the woods as it follows the creek into the watershed. It then begins the moderate climb up John's Mountain via a looping switchback. Near the top the trail drops to the base of and runs *behind* Keown Falls while a short spur climbs to the top of the cliff for a magnificent view of Furnace Valley and Horn Mountain. What makes the hike really special are the thousands of boulders that fill the area, typical of the ridge and valley area of northwest Georgia. For a longer hike, tie this trail in with the challenging 3.6-mile John's Mountain Trail.

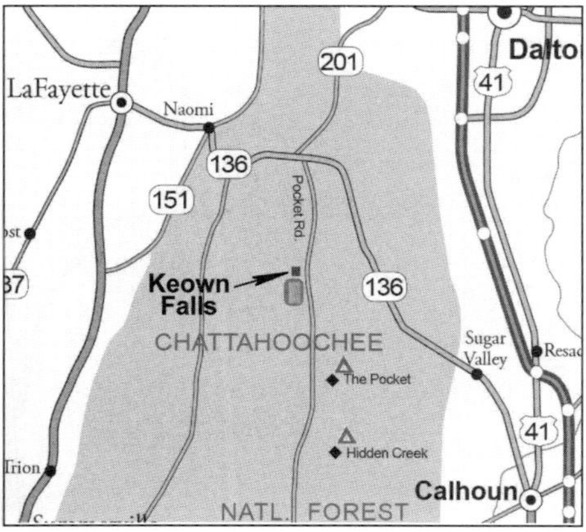

Directions: From LaFayette follow GA 146 east for 13.5 miles. Turn right onto Pocket Road and proceed approximately to FS 702 on the right. Follow the gravel road up to the parking area.

Sitton's Gulch Trail #56

Classic hike into the depths of Cloudland Canyon

Cloudland Canyon State Park
122 Cloudland Canyon Park Rd.
Rising Fawn, GA 30738
706.657.4050
www.gastateparks.org
GPS Coordinates:
34.8176°N / 085.4883°W

- **6.5 mile loop**
- **moderate to strenuous**
- **geologically and botanically rich area**

The bridge across Sitton Gulch Creek at the base of the stairs

Cloudland Canyon is one of the most interesting and dramatic geological landforms in Georgia, and like Tallulah Gorge in northeast Georgia, the best way to really experience it is to go "all in" as they say. The Sitton's Gulch Trail is a combination "in-and-out" and loop trail. It allows easy access to both canyon floor waterfalls before heading north along Sitton's Gulch Creek to an elongated loop. Don't underestimate this hike - you'll still have to tackle the 600 or so stairs (each way) to get in and out of the canyon plus the canyon floor has its own unique challenges.

The rewards are ample as the stream tumbles and races along the base of the canyon. Massive boulders and grey rock slabs litter the canyon floor and creek bed. Though it is a constant temptation, swimming is definitely not allowed. The canyon floor is cool, moist and shady throughout the hike and spring wildflowers can be dazzling. Check with the park for the latest trail conditions and be prepared to spend at least 3-4 hours on this amazing hike. Be sure to obtain an official park map at the visitor center near the park gate.

Directions: The park is located on GA 136 about 8 miles east of Trenton and I-59 exit 11, and about 18 miles west of LaFayette.

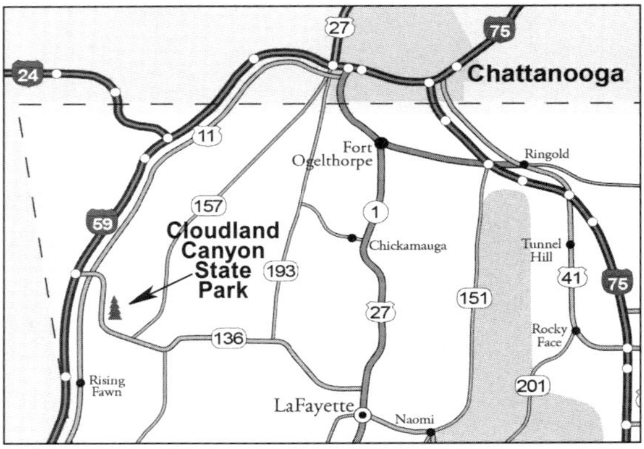

#57 Chattooga River Trail

Discover a gem of the elusive "Deliverance River"

Dick's Creek Ledge from the brink of Dick's Creek Falls

Chattooga Ranger District
Chattahoochee National Forest
706.754.6221

- **20 miles in Georgia**
- **moderate hiking**
- **check USFS regulations for backpacker camping**

The Chattooga River Trail is a favorite hiking destination for visitors to the northeast corner of the state. Rabun County is home to 20 miles of the trail before it crosses over onto the South Carolina side of the river and continues north for 12 miles up to Ellicott Rock at the junction of NC, SC and GA. Ironically, the trail stays alongside the river for only a fraction of its length in Rabun County. While it does remain almost entirely within the 1/4 mile protected Wild and Scenic River corridor, it spends most of its course along the lower slopes of the forest out of sight of the legendary river. This is not to suggest that the trail doesn't offer its delights.

There are two primary sections in Rabun County. Beginning at the U.S. 76 bridge east of Clayton the trail snakes 10 miles up to a junction with Sandy Ford Road (off Warwoman Road). About 20% of the trail is actually along the river offering beautiful views of the splashing waterway. One of the highlights is a scenic 1.5-mile section which closely parallels the riverbanks. This portion provides easy access to numerous sandy beaches and splashing shoals. Primitive camping sites abound.

Above Sandy Ford Road the trail intersects with the Bartram Trail coming in from Warwoman Dell near Clayton. The combined trails extend another 10 miles up to GA 28 (Russell bridge) where the trail crosses over onto the South Carolina side of the river. Highlights on this section include the short spur trail out to beautiful Dick's Creek Falls and Dick's Creek ledge, a Class IV rapid (see photo above).

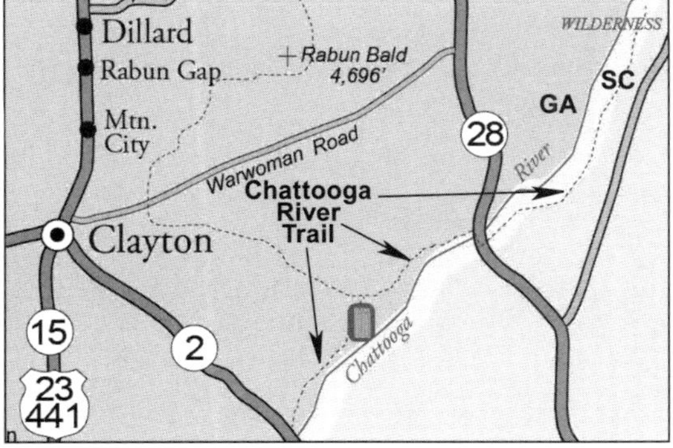

Bartram Trail #58

Retracing the path of the famous 18th century naturalist

Chattooga Ranger District
Chattahoochee National Forest
706.754.6221

- **37 miles in Georgia**
- **moderate to strenuous hiking**
- **day or overnight trips**

Rabun County is blessed with three legendary "long trails" either within or along its rugged boundaries. Besides the Appalachian Trail and Chattooga River Trail, the historic Bartram Trail winds through the county for 37 scenic miles. The trail follows the route of famed 18th century naturalist William Bartram who explored the region from 1773 to 1777. Without the luxuries of roads and maps, Bartram explored a tremendous portion of 8 southern states. The Bartram Trail today totals approximately 115 miles and has been designated a National Recreation Trail.

The Georgia portion lies within beautiful Rabun County and includes some wildly differing scenery. The toughest portion of the trail is the northern one-third which crosses the NC line near Sky Valley and climbs to the magnificent open summit of 4,696' Rabun Bald for a spectacular 360° view of the surrounding region. The Bartram then makes an undulating trek southwest over a series of peaks and gaps past two pretty waterfalls to Warwoman Dell just 2 miles east of Clayton on Warwoman Road.

The middle segment traverses a series of low ridges southeast from Warwoman Dell for nearly 10 miles to a junction with the Chattooga River Trail near Sandy Ford.

The final segment is 9.5 miles in length and closely parallels the Chattooga River northeast to the Hwy. 28 bridge where the trail crosses into South Carolina. This section features a scenic West Fork Chattooga River crossing on a dramatic footbridge. Detailed maps are available.

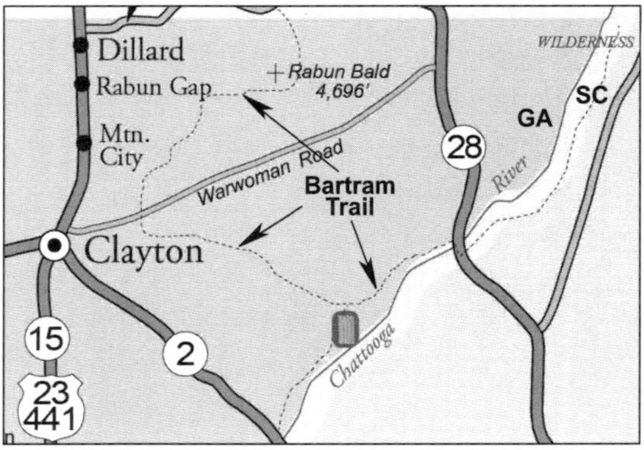

#59 Benton MacKaye Trail

A path honoring the father of the Appalachian Trail

Blue Ridge Ranger District
Chattahoochee National Forest
Phone: 706.754.6928

- **80 miles in Georgia**
- **moderate to strenuous hiking**
- **day or overnight trips**
- **waterfalls and scenic river crossing via suspension bridge**

Benton MacKaye (1879-1975) was a forester and conservationist who first envisioned the Appalachian Trail. Eighty miles of this challenging 287-mile footpath named for MacKaye arc across the North Georgia mountains. The path closely follows MacKaye's original vision of the AT as entering Georgia through the rugged Cohutta mountains. The path shares its starting point with the AT atop 3,782' Springer Mountain near Amicalola Falls State Park. In brief, the trail shares the AT pathway until reaching Three Forks where the Benton MaKaye Trail winds north, then turns sharply west just south of Blue Ridge, then bends north and courses through the Cohuttas before entering Tennessee.

Highlights of the Benton MacKaye Trail include Long Creek Falls near Three Forks, Fall Branch Falls and a magnificent 200+ foot suspension bridge over the scenic Toccoa River. The BMT features some fairly serious grades but most of it falls within the moderate category.

There is relatively good road access to the trail throughout its course in Georgia including two trail crossings on GA 60 between Suches and Morganton, and Highway 76 south of Blue Ridge. There are actually ten sections in Georgia which can be hiked individually or combined for a longer hike. A good overview of the sections can be found online at: www.bmta.org. Here you can select a section and get a free download of a detailed mile-by-mile description and trail profile.

There are a number of excellent publications detailing this footpath and a great deal of detailed information can be gathered online. Because of the confusing nature of this area and the many trails that lace this region, it is mandatory that anyone attempting the BMT have a reliable publication with maps. Perhaps the best is *Hiking the Benton MacKaye Trail* by veteran North Georgia outdoor writer Tim Homan (Peachtree Publishers).

Duncan Ridge Trail #60

One of North Georgia's most strenuous trails

Blue Ridge Ranger District
Chattahoochee National Forest
Phone: 706.754.6928

- **31 miles**
- **experienced hikers only**
- **strenuous rating**
- **combine with AT for 60 mile loop hike**

The 31-mile Duncan Ridge Trail has earned the reputation as one of Georgia's most strenuous footpaths. The path follows its namesake, Duncan Ridge, one of the longest continuous ridges that breaks from the main Blue Ridge mountain chain. The southern end of the trail begins near Three Forks along FS 58 and the Appalachian Trail near Long Creek Falls. The path winds northeast from here sharing its first 15 miles with the Benton MacKaye Trail. After crossing the beautiful Toccoa River via a dramatic 265' suspension bridge the trail crosses GA 60, one of only 2 major road crossings in its entire length.

North of GA 60 at Rhodes Mountain (2,985') the Duncan Ridge Trail turns sharply east and actually begins to traverse its namesake ridge as it negotiates a steep series of ascents and descents through Fish Gap (3,070'), Akin Mountain (3,540'), and Mulky Gap (2,795'). Several miles beyond Mulky Gap it runs alongside FS 39 (Duncan Ridge Road) before mounting strenuous ascents of both Wildcat Knob (3,927') and Coosa Bald (4,280'). The trail joins with Vogel State Park's Coosa Backcountry Trail before making a final climb up Slaughter Mountain (4,458') then descending to its endpoint at Slaughter Gap (3,920'). Many seasoned hikers continue from this point south along the AT back to Three Forks which works out to be a challenging 60-mile +/- hike.

Updated maps are mandatory for this trail - it traverses some of North Georgia's wildest country. Honestly gauge your fitness and experience level before attempting this hike!

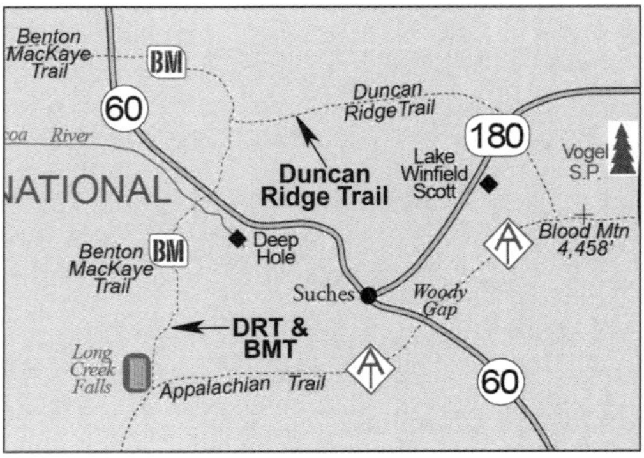

#61 Pinhoti Trail

Prelude to the AT is actually Georgia's longest footpath

Conasauga Ranger District
Chattahoochee National Forest
Phone: 706.695.6736

- **140 miles in northwest Georgia**
- **ends at Benton MacKaye Trail**
- **combination of trail, forest service roads and paved roads**

This one-page description of the 335-mile Pinhoti National Recreation Trail is really meant to just whet the appetite of the hiker looking to expand his or her "check-off" list. Most people familiar with Georgia trails seem oblivious to the fact that the Pinhoti Trail (Cherokee for "turkey home") is the longest trail in Georgia. Checking in at a total length of 140 miles in northwest Georgia (plus nearly 200 miles in Alabama) this trail is sure to garner more attention in the coming years. The trail is one component of a network of Appalachian Trail "connectors" which was a part of Benton MacKaye's early vision for the AT.

Georgia's section of this interesting pathway begins at the Alabama line in Polk County and curves northeast into the Armuchee ridges of the Chattahoochee National Forest west of Calhoun. The pathway crosses the valley section of northwest Georgia before entering the Cohutta wilderness region and joining the Benton MacKaye Trail around the 70-mile mark (distance from Springer Mountain) near Blue Ridge. One of the biggest problems with the Georgia section, particularly the middle section near Dalton, is that a tremendous amount of the "trail" actually utilizes the narrow or seemingly non-existent shoulders of paved roads and highways. In other words the Pinhoti Trail is great in theory but at this point is not where its founders would like as far as being a completed trail.

Don't be discouraged and think that there's not some good hiking though. Frequented sections include those around James H. "Sloppy" Floyd State Park, the Armuchee Ridges region and the Cohuttas. With a little homework you just may discover Georgia's newest "long trail." Here are a few websites you can visit to find out more:

www.georgiapinhoti.org
www.alabamatrail.org
www.Pinhotitrailalliance.org

Appalachian Trail #62

Legendary trail with great overnight and day hikes

Blue Ridge Ranger District
Chattahoochee National Forest
Phone: 706.754.6928
Chattooga Ranger District
706.754.6221

- **75+ miles in Georgia**
- **moderate to strenuous**
- **numerous day hike options**

The legendary Appalachian Trail has a special place in the heart of Georgians who love the great outdoors. This world-renowned 2,100-mile footpath starts in North Georgia a little over an hour north of Atlanta. Each spring hundreds (if not thousands) of "thru-hikers" set out from the summit of Springer Mountain (3,782') near Dahlonega intent on living the dream of walking along the lofty spine of the Appalachians all the way to Mt. Katahdin in Maine. The high point along Georgia's portion of the AT is atop Blood Mountain (4.496') while the lowest elevation is at Dick's Creek Gap (2,675') along U.S. 76 between Clayton and Hiawassee.

The Appalachian Trail is marked with 2" x 6" vertical white rectangular blazes for its entire 2,100-mile length. Double-blazes mark turns, while side trails of note are marked in blue. Most water sources have signs or markings of some sort. Generally speaking it's pretty tough to get lost or confused on the trail as signage is good and there are usually a respectable number of hikers out on the trail in the warmer months.

If you are looking to mount a backpacking trip on the trail, whether overnight or for an extended period, there are literally dozens of books, maps and internet sources to help plan your route, itinerary and logistics. For purposes of this guide we will divide the trail into sections and provide just a few of the highlights. Because trail usage is heavy please familiarize yourself with AT guidelines such as:

- travel only on foot and stay on the footpath
- pack it in; pack it out! please keep the AT clean for everyone
- travel in small groups; 4-6 is ideal, 25 is the maximum.
- camp only in established sites, and in groups of 10 or less
- use a backpacking stove rather than building a campfire

Notable features by section/mile; miles from Springer Mountain

Springer Mtn. - Hightower Gap - 9 miles

Springer Mountain shelter - mile 0.2; FS 42 - mile 0.9; Stover Creek shelter - mile 2.5; Three Forks - mile 4.1; Hawk Mountain Shelter - mile 7.6; Hightower Gap, FS 42/69 - mile 8.1

Hightower Gap - Woody Gap - 11.9 miles

Horse Gap - mile 10.0; Cooper Gap, FS 42/80 - mile 11.6; Justice Creek - mile 13.6; Blackwell Creek - mile 14.3; Gooch Gap Shelter - mile 16.1; Gooch Gap, FS 42 - mile 16.4; Woody Gap - mile 20

Woody Gap - Neel's Gap - 10.7 miles

Woody Gap - mile 20; Lunsford Gap - mile 20.7; Big Cedar Mountain - mile 21.5; Jarrard Gap - mile 25.3; Bird Gap - mile 26.7; Blood Mountain, Blood Mountain shelter - mile 28.3; Byron Reece Spur Trail - mile 29.8; Neels Gap, U.S. 19/129 - mile 30.7

Neel's Gap - Hogpen Gap - 6.4 miles

Neel's Gap - mile 30.7; Bull Gap - mile 31.8; Cowrock Mountain - mile 35.4; Tesnatee Gap, GA 348 (Russell Hwy) - mile 36.2; Hogpen Gap, GA 348 - mile 37.1

- continued on following page

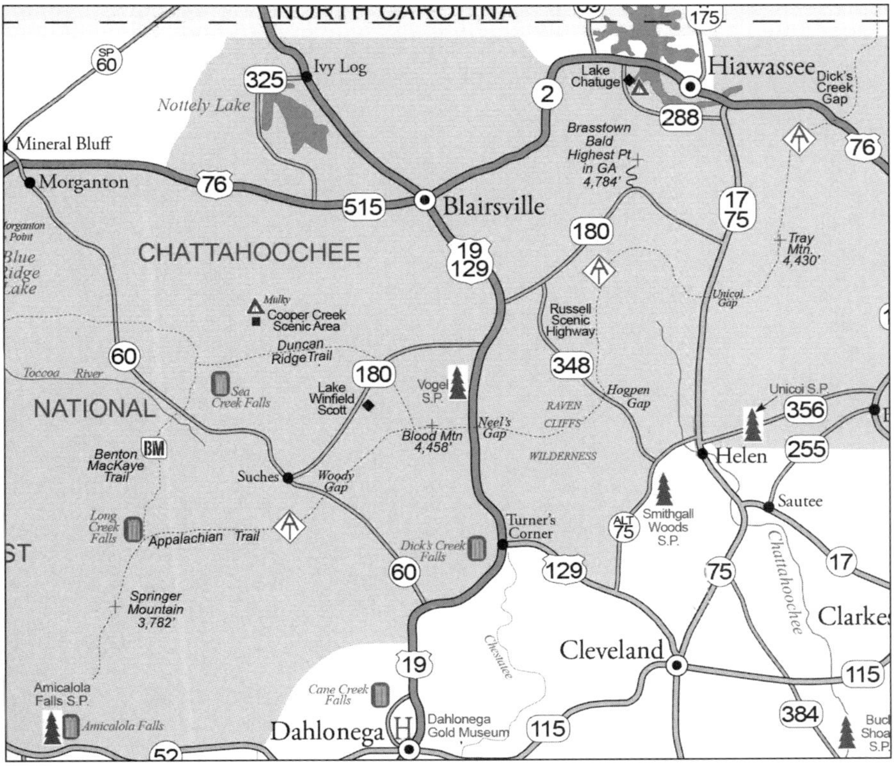

Hogpen Gap - Unicoi Gap - 13.6 miles

Hogpen Gap, GA 348 - mile 37.1; Low Gap Shelter - mile 41.3; Poplar Stomp Gap - mile 42.7; Chattahoochee Gap - mile 46.3; Blue Mountain shelter - mile 48.5; Unicoi Gap, GA 17/75 - mile 50.7

Unicoi Gap - Tray Gap - 6.2 miles

Unicoi Gap, GA 17/75 - mile 50.7; Rocky Mountain - mile 52; Tray Mountain Road, FS 79 - mile 54.1; Tray Gap, FS 79 - mile 55.1

Tray Gap - Dick's Creek Gap - 11.7 miles

Tray Gap, FS 79 - mile 55.1; Tray Mountain shelter - mile 56.2; Sassafras Gap - mile 60.7; Addis Gap - mile 61.5; Deep Gap shelter - mile 63.3; McClure Gap - mile 64.4; Dick's Creek Gap, U.S. 76 - mile 66.8

Dick's Cr. Gap - Bly Gap (NC line) - 15.6 miles

Dick's Creek Gap, U.S. 76 - mile 66.8; Plumorchard Gap shelter - mile 71.1; campsite - mile 73.4; NC / GA line - mile 75.4

5

USFS CAMPGROUNDS & RECREATION AREAS

Lake Winfield Scott Recreation Area #63

One of Georgia's most scenic mountain lakes

Lake Winfield Scott Rec. Area, - Union County
Chattahoochee National Forest
706.747.3816
GPS coordinates:
34.7406°N / 83.9757°W

- **camping & picknicking**
- **swimming & fishing**
- **boating (electric motors only)**
- **hiking**
- **user fee required**

One of Georgia's loftiest mountain lakes (elevation 2,854') is the centerpiece of this popular recreation area in beautiful Union County. Named for General Winfield Scott who served in the U.S. Army for over 40 years and managed the removal of the Cherokee in the infamous "Trail of Tears," this 18-acre lake is the source of Cooper Creek, long considered one of Georgia's most productive trout streams.

Tucked away between Vogel State Park and Suches, Lake Winfield Scott is a great alternate base for Blood Mountain hikes. In addition to camping, swimming (cold!), fishing and picnicking, several excellent hiking trails originate here. The 0.4-mile **Winfield Scott Trail** circles the lake, while the **Slaughter Creek Trail** (2.7 miles) and the **Jarrard Gap Trail** (1.2 miles) climb from the recreation area to the busy Appalachian Trail. These trails create several possible routes for a Blood Mountain ascent.

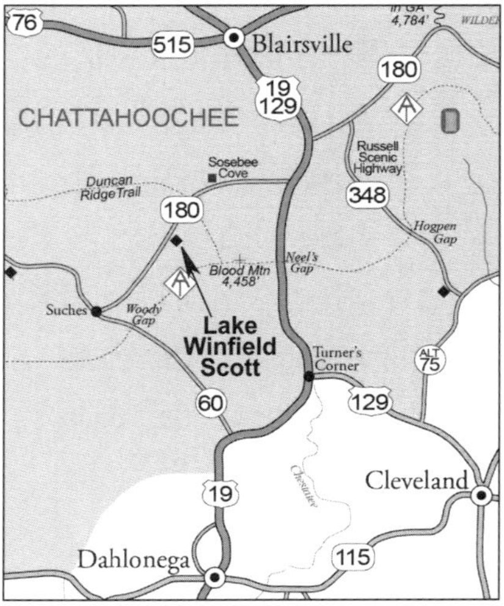

Directions: Lake Winfield Scott is located on scenic GA 180 about halfway between Suches and Vogel State Park. GA 180 is quite popular with motorcyclists, especially the "crotch rocket" variety. There have been many injuries and some deaths involving motorcycles on this road.

#64 Woody Gap Recreation Area

Roadside picnic area and several great AT hikes

Woody Gap Recreation Area
Lumpkin/Union County line
Chattahoochee National Forest
706.747.3816
GPS coordinates:
34.4066°N / 83.5997°W

- **scenic picnic area**
- **AT trailhead**
- **several day hike options**

AT marker at Woody Gap

Pretty Woody Gap (elevation 3,160') is a strategically positioned Appalachian Trail access point located just south of Suches. It is the first major highway crossing as the Appalachian Trail heads north from Springer Mountain. While plenty of serious AT "through hikers" pass this way, it is also a good starting point for several enjoyable day hikes. The picnic area is quite nice as well, so even if you don't intend to hike, Woody Gap is a nice spot to stop, enjoy the view, or just picnic for awhile.

The easiest day-hike involves a 1.2-mile hike (one way) north along the AT to several overlooks atop Big Cedar Mountain which offer wonderful views to the east. There is some climbing but nothing serious.

Looking for more? From Woody Gap you can follow the AT for 5.7 miles to Jarrard Gap, then turn west and descend 1.2 miles to Lake Winfield Scott, or continue another 3.2 miles combing to the lofty summit of Blood Mountain (4,461'). The next highway crossing is at Neel's Gap, another 2.5 miles distant.

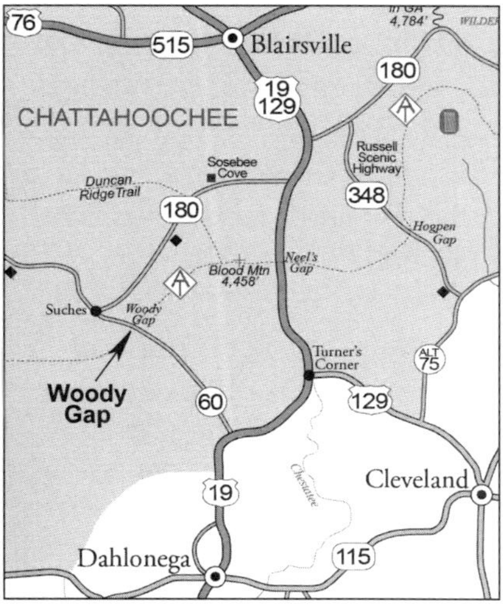

Directions: Woody Gap is located along GA 60 approximately 14 miles north of Dahlonega, about 3 miles south of Suches.

Chestatee Overlook #65

Roadside picnic overlooks Blood Mountain Cove

Blue Ridge Ranger District
Chattahoochee National Forest
GPS coordinates:
34.6648°N / 83.9835°W

- **roadside pulloff**
- **scenic overlook of Blood Mountain Cove**

In round numbers, GA 60 traverses about 40 miles in its journey from Dahlonega to Morganton, and this is one of the most scenic stretches of highway in all of North Georgia. In fact, the road is a little too dramatic for some. Drivers must negotiate hundreds of curves along this narrow stretch of asphalt. There is plenty of great scenery but the road commands your full attention. This is especially true of motorcyclists who flock to the area to test their skills on the hairpin curves of GA 60 and GA 180.

There are views aplenty but relatively few spots to safely exit your vehicle and really enjoy them. Chestatee overlook is one of those spots. It's pretty basic - just a small overlook with a big view. Not long ago there were 3 picnic tables here but no more. This spot is pretty far away from the crowds and is a nice place for a picnic or an opportunity to get out of your vehicle and stretch your legs while you enjoy the view north into beautiful Blood Mountain Cove. It's one of the few north-facing overlooks along GA 60.

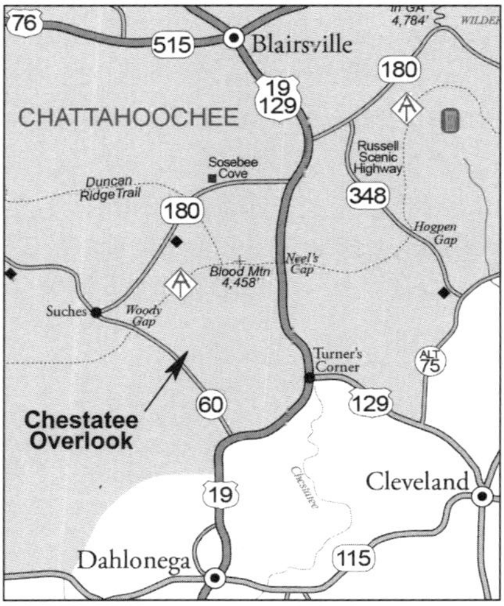

Directions: Chestatee Overlook is located approximately 13 miles north of Dahlonega on GA 60 (just a few hundred yards past the road which turns off to Dockery Lake).

#66 Dockery Lake Recreation Area

Tiny lake offers some big recreational opportunities

Blue Ridge Ranger District
Chattahoochee National Forest
Phone: 706.754.6928
GPS coordinates:
34.6641°N / 83.9812°W

- **excellent trout fishing**
- **camping & hiking**
- **picnic shelters**
- **Appalachian Trail access**
- **user fee required**
- **open seasonally (contact USFS for dates)**

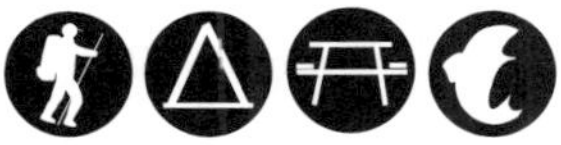

Beautiful Dockery Lake is a peaceful 6-acre lake hidden in a sea of deep green forest. Located at a cool elevation of 2,388' Dockery's cold, clear waters attract trout anglers while its secluded camping (only 11 campsites with limited facilities) and picnic area (6 lake front picnic tables) offer plenty of peace and quiet in a tranquil, scenic setting.

There are two hiking paths of note at Dockery Lake Recreation Area. Most everyone will want to tackle the 0.5-mile **Lakeshore Trail** during their visit. It makes an easy loop around the lake and as a bonus this trail is handicap accessible.

For those who really want to get out and stretch the legs the **Dockery Lake Trail** will provide a bit of a challenge. This delightful trail stretches 3.4 scenic miles along an old logging road northward to Miller Gap (elevation 2,980') on the Appalachian Trail. Overall there is about a 500' change in elevation, including a steep descent to Pigeon Roost Creek (around 2,000' elevation) followed by a steep 0.5-mile ascent before the grade eases somewhat. The Dockery Lake Trail

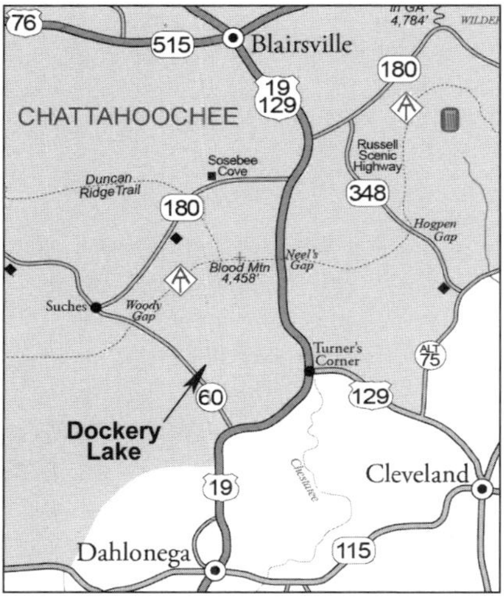

meets the Appalachian Trail at a point 3 miles north of Woody Gap and 8.6 miles south of Neel's Gap on U.S. 19/129.

This is a nice trail to see dozens of species of flowering shrubs and wildflowers. Mountain laurel and several species of rhododendron are prominent with a wide variety of wildflowers decorating the forest floor in the spring and summer.

Wildlife sightings are quite common as well. A multitude of bird species are found here and deer are frequently sighted in the area. Black bears are also quite common in the area but are not seen as often, preferring to do most of their hunting at night.

Note: For such a secluded location, Dockery Lake receives a great deal of visitation during the tourist season particularly on weekends. Plan your trip accordingly.

Directions: From Dahlonega, take GA 60 north for about 13 miles. Turn right onto FS 654 (Dockery Lake Road) and follow the gravel road approximately one mile to the parking area.

#67 Frank Gross Campground

Secluded campground offers great fishing options

Blue Ridge Ranger District
Chattahoochee National Forest
706.745.6928
GPS coordinates:
34.7014°N / 84.1494°W

- **small secluded campground**
- **trout fishing**
- **lake fishing closeby**
- **close to Appalachian Trail**
- **close to Chattahoochee National Fish Hatchery**
- **user fee required**

Rhododendron bloom

Frank Gross campground is wonderfully secluded deep within the Chattahoochee National Forest. If you're used to big campgrounds with lots of people, you'll find Frank Gross a welcome change. The campground is located at approximately 2,300' elevation and is nestled along the clear trout waters of splashing Rock Creek. The campground features 9 camping sites with one vault facility for disabled persons, and it offers all the comforts of home: picnic tables, drinking water and 2 chemical toilets. The campground will accommodate trailers up to 22 feet.

Fishing is the main activity in camp, but if stream fishing isn't what you came for simply drive 1.7 miles farther west to pretty 13-acre Rock Creek Lake which is managed by the nearby Chattahoochee National Fish Hatchery. Both the creek and lake are regularly stocked with rainbow trout.

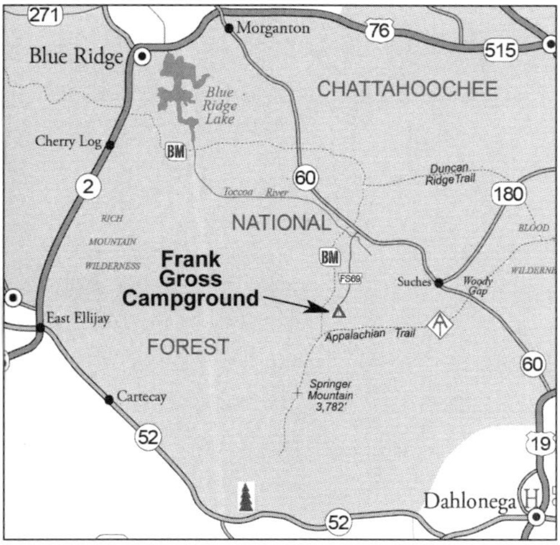

Directions: From Dahlonega follow GA 60 north for 27 miles. Turn left (heading south) onto FS 69 (Fish Hatchery Road). Follow the gravel road for 5 miles to the campground.

Deep Hole Recreation Area #68

Located on the beautiful Toccoa River

Blue Ridge Ranger District
Chattahoochee National Forest
706.745.6928
GPS coordinates:
34.739723°N / 84.140072°W

- **excellent trout fishing**
- **small campground**
- **close to major hiking trails**
- **user fee required**

Forest meets river in the placid waters of the Toccoa River at Deep Hole

Deep Hole Recreation Area is located along a sharp bend in the beautiful Toccoa River, the major feeder stream for Lake Blue Ridge. "Toccoa" is said to mean *beautiful* in the native Cherokee language, and this stunning mountain stream certainly lives up to its name. Eight campsites are located a stone's throw from the river providing the perfect setting for an enjoyable camping trip. Like all USFS campgrounds there are rules and anyone planning to camp should take a look before committing.

The calm deep waters of the Toccoa River provide great fishing with rainbow trout, brown trout and bass being the main menu items. Deep Hole is the starting point for the 13.8-mile Toccoa River Canoe Trail. This magnificent stream is great for beginners with generally easy whitewater.

There's plenty of good hiking closeby as well including the Benton Mackaye, Duncan Ridge and Appalachian Trails just a short drive away.

Directions: From Dahlonega take GA 60 north for 27 miles. Coming south from Morganton take GA 60 south for 16 miles.

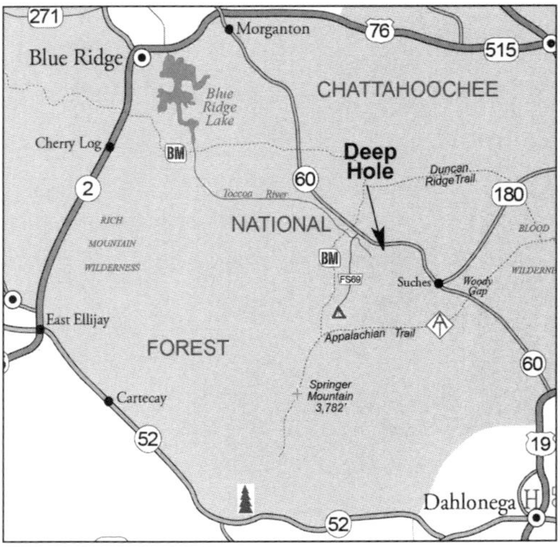

#69 Cooper Creek Scenic Area

Camping, hiking, fishing set amidst a splendid natural area

Blue Ridge Ranger District
Chattahoochee National Forest
Phone: 706.754.6928
706.754.6221
GPS coordinates:
34.76398°N / 84.06686°W

- **hiking trails**
- **botanically rich area**
- **wildlife viewing**
- **trout fishing**
- **2 USFS campgrounds**

Pristine 1,240-acre Cooper Creek Scenic Area is a favorite destination for campers, trout anglers, and hunters. Hikers will find plenty to like here as well. The scenic area is virtually surrounded by the vast Cooper Creek Wildlife Management Area so there's no doubt that hunting and fishing are quite popular. The namesake stream, Cooper Creek, flows approximately 2 miles east-to-west through the center of this pristine Chattahoochee National Forest preserve, offering trout fishermen a top-notch mountain stream to test their angling skills.

Elevations within Cooper Creek Scenic Area range from roughly 2,000' along the creek to approximately 3,000' atop Yellow Mountain. Camping is quite popular here with 2 USFS camping areas, Mulky and Cooper Creek located near the northwest corner of the area . Mulky features 11 bare-bones campsites while Cooper Creek has 17. The camping sites at Cooper Creek can handle tents or trailers up to 22 feet.

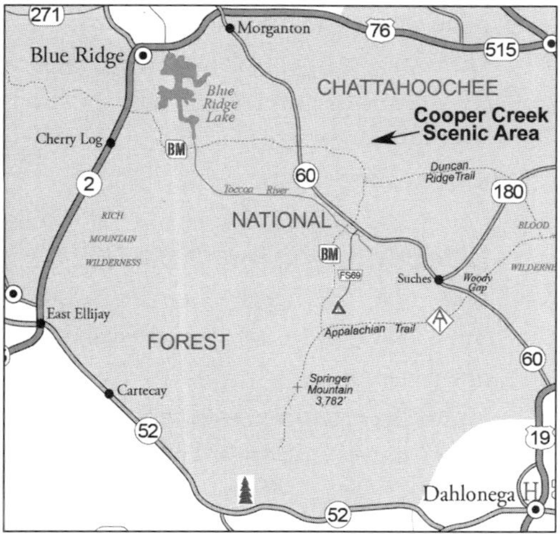

Much of Cooper Creek Scenic Area is believed to be virgin forest, never touched by logging that was prevalent in the early 20th century. Vast stands of enormous hemlocks and tulip poplars can be found throughout the scenic area.

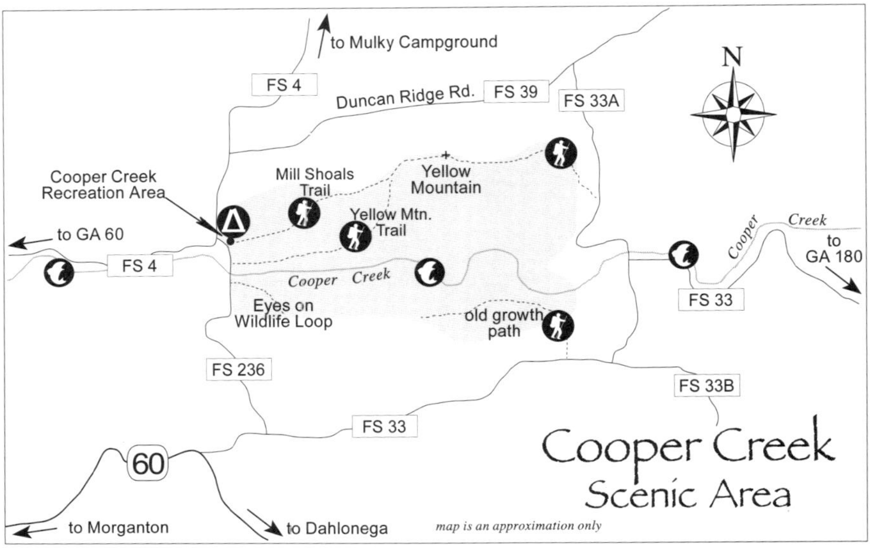

Hikers who traverse the area have a chance to see some of Georgia's finest tall timber.

Hiking: Several maintained hiking trails push into the Cooper Creek Scenic Area. The popular **Mill Shoals Trail** winds 2.4 miles across the northwest corner. In the past this trail has been somewhat poorly marked so pay close attention as you hike.

Another option is the 3.6-mile **Yellow Mountain Trail** which primarily follows the ridge line to the summit of 2,963' Yellow Mountain. Because of the appreciable change in elevation this trail is rated as moderate.

Connecting these 2 trails is the 0.4-mile **Cooper Creek Trail**. To the south an interesting trail often referred to as the **"old-growth path"** heads west into some of the oldest and most impressive stands of timber in the scenic area.

The 1.6-mile **Eyes on Wildlife Loop Trail** is an easy-to-moderate path featuring plants that have thrived since salvage logging operations and prescribed burns were performed; this has allowed more sunlight to reach the forest floor and provided native wildlife with more places to feed.

The 0.9-mile **Shope Gap Trail** ties in with the Yellow Mountain Trail, some 1.3 miles from the trailhead. Rated moderate to strenuous, this trail runs north and intersects Duncan Ridge Road north of the scenic area.

Directions: From Dahlonega, take GA 60 north for 27 miles. Turn right onto FS 4 and proceed approximately 6 miles to Cooper Creek Recreation Area. FS 4 is approximately 16 miles south of Morganton on GA 60.

#70 Andrews Cove Campground

Tiny campground on Andrews Creek and AT spur trail

Chattooga Ranger District
Chattahoochee National Forest
706.747.3816
GPS coordinates:
34.7782°N / 83.7375°W

- **small campground**
- **trout fishing**
- **AT connector trail**
- **open seasonally**
- **user fee required**

Tiny Andrews Cove Recreation Area is located just 10 minutes north of busy Alpine Helen but is virtually a world away from the traffic and congestion of the bustling tourist town. Andrews Cove has only 10 campsites, so it retains a bit of an intimate feel. Located in a heavily wooded cove just south of Unicoi Gap and the Appalachian Trail, it offers a great deal in terms of location. Splashing Andrews Creek tumbles through the cove creating a wonderful atmosphere for camping.

Hikers wishing to access the Appalachian Trail directly can take the 2-mile Andrews Cove Trail northeast (uphill) to a junction with the AT at Indian Grave Gap along FS 283. This portion of the AT is 1.7 miles east of Unicoi Gap (GA 17/75) and about 2.5 miles from the Tray Mountain summit. In the grand scheme of things Andrews Cove is small and simple, but try it once and you'll discover why it's a repeat destination for many North Georgia campers.

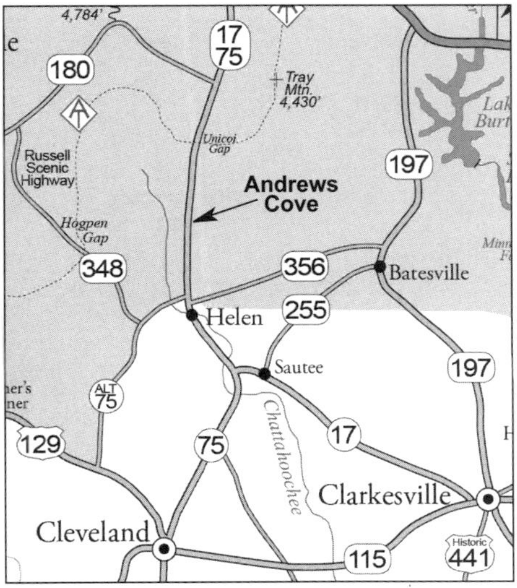

Directions: Proceed north from Helen on GA 17/75 for approximately 5 miles. Andrews Cove is located in a hairpin curve on the right.

Upper Chattahoochee River #71

Campground located near the famous river's headwaters

The fledgling Chattahoochee squeezes through a narrow sluice upstream of the Upper Chattahoochee campground.

Chattooga Ranger District
Chattahoochee National Forest
706.754.6221
GPS coordinates:
34.78659°N / 83.78297°W

- **beautiful campground**
- **trout fishing**
- **Horse Trough Falls**
- **picnicking**
- **user fee required**

The Chattahoochee River, or *river of the painted rock* as the native Cherokee knew it, is one of Georgia's largest and well known waterways. This famous stream originates a short distance from this scenic recreation area adjacent to the rugged Mark Trail Wilderness. The Upper Chattahoochee Recreation Area features a serene campground situated at a cool 2,260' elevation. There are 34 sites total; 10 for tents only and 24 for tents or recreational vehicles. It's pretty basic but it's really nice.

Trout fishing can be enjoyed on the fledgling Chattahoochee River which flows through the camping area. Scenic FS 44 follows the river for portions of the ride up to the camping area. As a bonus, beautiful Horse Trough Falls is a several hundred yard walk from the upper end of the camping loop.

Directions: Easiest route: Take GA 17/75 north from Helen for 9.4 miles. Turn left onto FS 44 and drive 4.8 bumpy miles to the recreation area. Most scenic route: Follow GA 17/75 north from Helen for 1.5 miles and turn left onto GA 75 ALT. Immediately turn right at the Chattahoochee Church onto Poplar Stump Road which soon turns into FS 44. It's a long 10 mile ride to the recreation area, but it's well worth the hassle.

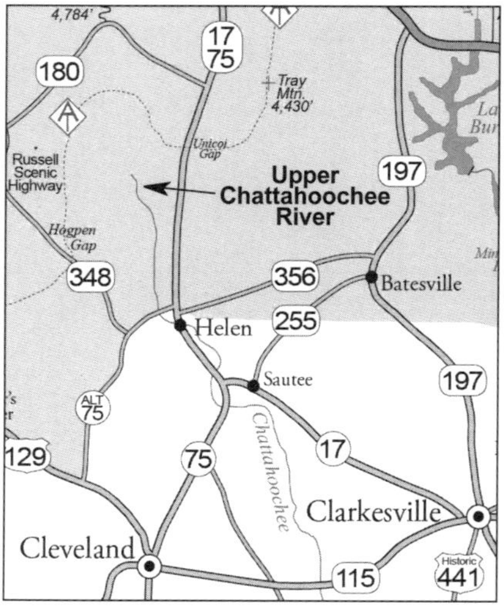

#72 Desoto Falls Scenic Area

Camping and a scenic hike to two pretty waterfalls

Blue Ridge Ranger District
Chattahoochee National Forest
706.745.6928
GPS coordinates:
34.721202°N / 83.917409°W

- **2 small waterfalls**
- **beautiful campground**
- **picnic area**
- **trout fishing**
- **USFS fee area**

Upper falls

Historical accounts hint that legendary Spanish explorer Hernando Desoto visited the northeast Georgia region in the 1500s, long before white settlers ventured into the wild and unforgiving region. Legend has it that a piece of Spanish armor was found many years later in the area which today is known as Desoto Falls Scenic Area.

Visitors can enjoy camping, fishing and hiking in this cool, scenic 650-acre preserve including 2 small, picturesque waterfalls in the narrow Frogtown Creek watershed. To visit these waterfalls, follow the footpath that leads from the day-use parking area to a small footbridge over splashing Frogtown Creek. From here, turn right and follow an easy trail 0.7 mile upstream along Frogtown Creek to a multi-tiered waterfall on a small Frogtown tributary creek. Retrace your steps to the trailhead footbridge and continue straight ahead for several hundred yards along a short loop that climbs up to a smaller 25' cascade (which can virtually disappear during dry spells).

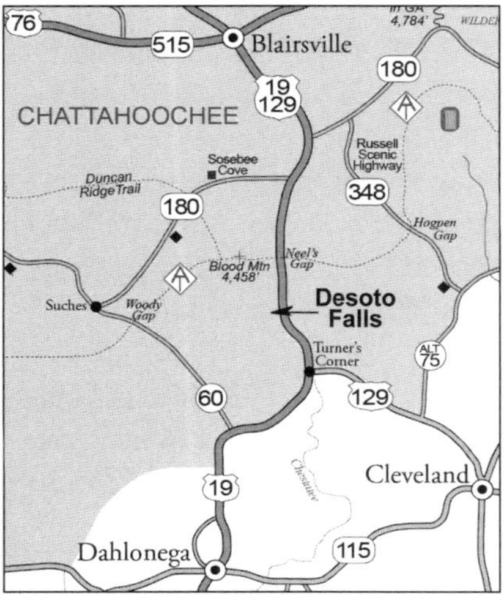

Directions: Desoto Falls Scenic Area is located on U.S. 19/129 approximately 15 miles north of Cleveland (4 miles north of Turner's Corner).

Warwoman Dell Recreation Area #73

Quiet recreation area has deep historical roots

Chattooga Ranger District
Chattahoochee National Forest
706.754.6221
GPS coordinates:
34.8820362°N / 83.350992°W

- **beautiful picnic spot**
- **nature trail**
- **Bartram Trail access**
- **waterfalls closeby**
- **historical interest**

Warwoman Dell was developed in the 1930s depression years by the Civilian Conservation Corps (CCC). It was originally used as a CCC camp, and the area has a rich and colorful history. Be sure to read the information board in the dell and the Bartram historical marker at the trail crossing on the highway. The dell is primarily a picnic area but hikers hold it in high esteem as well. A 0.4-mile **nature loop** winds through the grounds as does the well-known **Bartram Trail**. This challenging trail heads north from the dell for 13 miles to mighty Rabun Bald, Georgia's second highest peak. Go east for 9 miles and you'll intersect the legendary Chattooga River near Sandy Ford. Take the Bartram Trail north across Warwoman Road for about 0.2 mile and you'll come face-to-face with playful Becky Branch Falls.

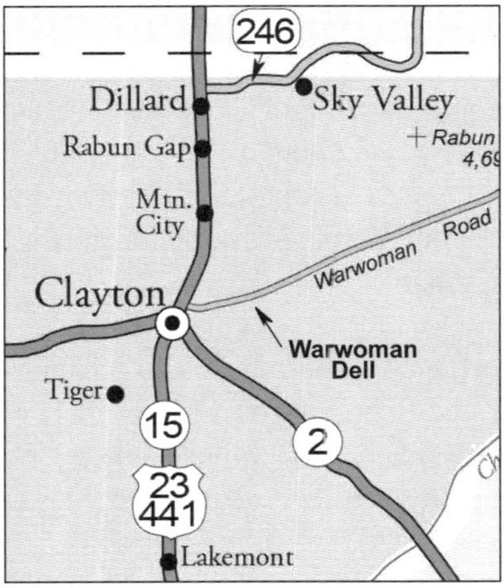

The ill-fated Blue Ridge Railroad attempted to construct a line from Charleston to Knoxville before the Civil War. Remains of this never-completed project are on the hillside just above the dell. Look for the stone steps that climb to the remains.

Directions: From U.S. 441 in Clayton, turn onto Warwoman Road at the Days Inn and proceed 2.4 miles to Warwoman Dell on the right.

#74 Rabun Beach Recreation Area

Camping and boating on magnificent Lake Rabun

Chattooga Ranger District
Chattahoochee National Forest
706.754.6221
GPS coordinates:
34.775767°N / 83.481299°W

- **2 large campgrounds**
- **picnicking by the lake**
- **swimming beach**
- **boating & fishing**
- **hiking trails**
- **user fee required**

Lake Rabun is considered one of the most beautiful mountain lakes in the Blue Ridge. This 825-acre gem is a popular summer resort known for its upscale homes and incredible natural beauty. Rabun Beach Recreation Area is located along the lake's northwestern shoreline and is home to the largest U.S. Forest Service campground in Georgia with 85 sites, most with water and electrical hookups.

The amenities here are impressive including a boat ramp and a popular swimming beach with bath house. An elevated platform about 100 feet from shore is a popular gathering spot for swimmers. The lake side picnic area is extremely nice as well. Hikers will appreciate the one-mile (one way) Joe Branch Trail in camping area #2 which leads to 2 pretty waterfalls - Panther Falls and Angel Falls.

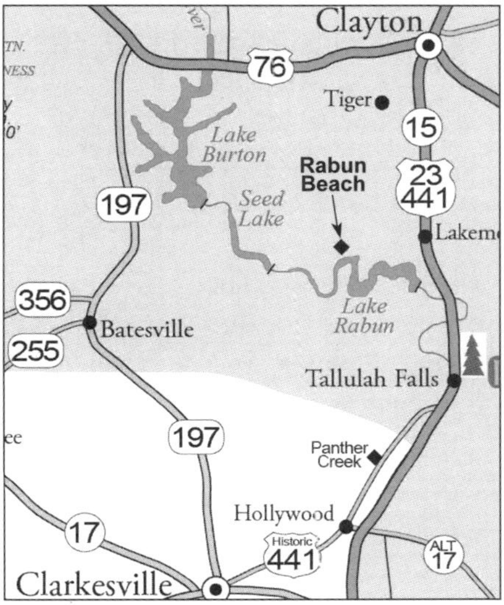

Directions: From the U.S. 441 bridge in Tallulah Falls drive 1.7 miles north and turn left onto Old 441. Proceed 2.4 miles and turn left onto Lake Rabun Road. Drive 4.5 miles to the recreation area.

Popcorn Overlook #75

Beautiful roadside views into the rugged Southern Nantahalas

Chattooga Ranger District
Chattahoochee National Forest
706.754.6221
GPS coordinates:
34.87482°N / 83.57460°W

- **scenic overlook**
- **picnicking**
- **Appalachian Trail access nearby**

The 25-mile drive along beautiful U.S. 76 from Clayton to Hiawassee features an incredible diversity of scenery. Initially the highway runs through narrow valleys dotted with farms and the occasional local business. Beyond a scenic crossing of sparkling Lake Burton the roadway climbs to the forested shoulders of peaks along the Rabun/ Towns County line where it briefly encounters the elusive Appalachian Trail.

Several miles prior to reaching the AT the highway passes the scenic Popcorn Overlook, a north-facing pull-off with excellent vistas into North Carolina's rugged Southern Nantahala Wilderness. The unusual name comes from a nearby trout stream, Popcorn Creek. The overlook is a nice location for a roadside picnic area on a pretty day. Late autumn afternoons are especially nice as the setting sun splashes the scene in vibrant colors.

Directions: The overlook is located about 12 miles west of Clayton on U.S. 441, just west of the GA 197 junction.

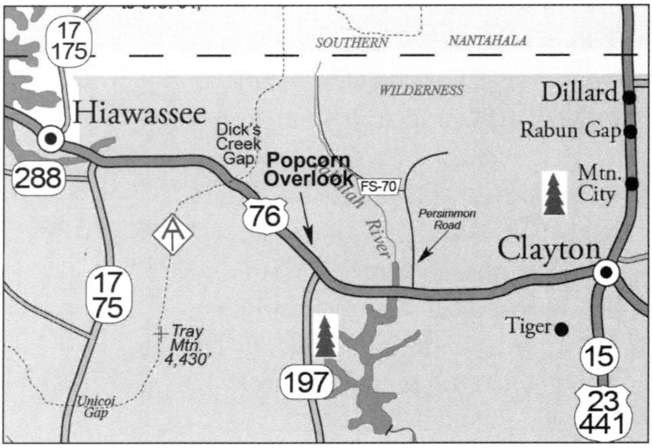

#76 Upper Tallulah Basin

Three scenic USFS campgrounds along the upper Tallulah

Chattooga Ranger District
Chattahoochee National Forest
706.754.6221
GPS coordinates:
34.927176°N / 83.543205°W
(Tallulah Campground)

- **3 campgrounds on the Tallulah River**
- **trout fishing**
- **local hiking trails**
- **scenic Rock Gorge**
- **waterfalls closeby**

Tallulah River cascades in the Rock Gorge

The area known today as Tate City was once a busy mining and logging settlement nestled far from civilization in an isolated valley at the southern base of lofty Standing Indian Mountain. The industry is gone but a handful of families still make their homes in this spectacular valley near the headwaters of the Tallulah River. The 9-mile drive along dramatic Tallulah River Road (FS 70) is alone worth the trip but there is much more to do and see in this remarkable area.

The most scenic part of the drive is a 3-mile stretch along the river through a section known as the Rock Gorge. The road hugs the river as it tumbles, crashes and surges around house-sized boulders and through narrow crevices over literally hundreds of small waterfalls and cascades. Above and below the gorge the Tallulah is relatively peaceful, attracting hundreds of trout fishermen, tubers, waders and swimmers who ply its cold, clear waters. There are literally dozens of nice spots to enjoy along the river.

Tiny Tate City with its picture-postcard scenery is located several miles north of the gorge. The fields and farms of Tate City abruptly end at the North Carolina state line where the valley becomes wild and narrow once more. Several miles north the road abruptly ends at a small parking area that access several trails. Three splendid U.S. Forest Service campgrounds are located along FS-70 (see next page) providing a great base of operations.

Directions: Starting in Clayton take U.S. 76 west for 8 miles. Turn left onto Persimmon Road and drive north for 4 miles. Turn left onto Tallulah River Road (FS-70). Your upper Tallulah adventure begins here.

USFS Campgrounds

Tallulah River Campground: Located one mile from Persimmon Road. Featuring 17 campsites at 2,080' elevation. Open seasonally.

Tate Branch Campground: Located 4 miles from Persimmon Road. Tate Branch has 16 campsites at 2,360' elevation. Open all year.

Sandy Bottom Campground: Sandy Bottom campground is located 5 miles from Persimmon Road a short distance downriver from Tate City. Sandy Bottom has 12 campsites at an elevation of 2,420'. Open seasonally.

Hiking Trails: This is a beautiful but rugged region and most of the hiking trails are challenging. There are a few easy hikes such as the **Coleman River Trail** (see "Classic Walks" section) which follows the Coleman River upstream into a narrow valley. This one mile trail (one way) is fairly easy. The trailhead is located along Tallulah River Road (FS 70) 1.7 miles from Persimmon Road.

Denton Branch Falls can be reached by an easy 0.25 mile stroll. The 0.25 trail to the falls begins at a dirt road 6.5 miles from Persimmon Road.

The fantastic Beech **Creek Trail** offers over 10 miles of highly scenic and challenging, hiking. This trail features several waterfalls and a steady but tiring ascent into the Beech Creek watershed. Because of its backcountry nature, length and elevation change, anyone wishing to tackle the Beech Creek loop as it is known should purchase a detailed map or guidebook to the area.

An easier option is a 4.5 mile in-and-out hike from the southern Beech Creek trailhead. It features pretty 200' High Falls. The lower trailhead is located 7.8 miles from Persimmon Road (about 0.4 mile north of the North Carolina state line).

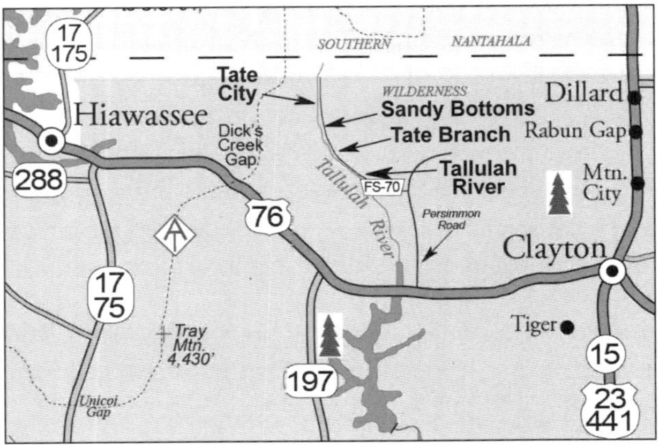

The upper trailhead is at the end of FS-70 just over a mile from the southern trailhead. Make sure you have a detailed guidebook or a good map before trying this one as well.

#77 Lake Chatuge Recreation Area

On the southern shoreline of 7,000-acre TVA lake

Dogwoods bloom against the backdrop of the lake

Blue Ridge Ranger District
Chattahoochee National Forest
706.745.6928
GPS coordinates:
34.9545°N / 83.7796°W

- **loop trail**
- **fishing & boating**
- **picnicking**
- **boat ramp**
- **user fee required**

Massive Lake Chatuge is a 7,000-acre Tennessee Valley Authority (TVA) impoundment that seemingly surrounds the Towns County city of Hiawassee. Situated at an altitude of 1,926', Chatuge is a massive lake that boasts hundreds of upscale homes along its shoreline as well as a number of marinas, parks, and restaurants. Lake Chatuge Recreation area is located just west of Hiawassee and though the campground was recently closed it still offers good lake access. If you like boating on big "open water" make your way north under the U.S. 76 bridge and the lake will open up in all its glory. The recreation area has its own boat ramp for fishermen and pleasure boaters. If you want to stretch your legs the 1.2-mile **Lake Chatuge Trail** winds around the peninsula. Check locally for boat rentals on Lake Chatuge.

Directions: Take U.S. 76 west from downtown Hiawassee for 2 miles. Turn left onto GA 288 and proceed one mile to the recreation area on the left.

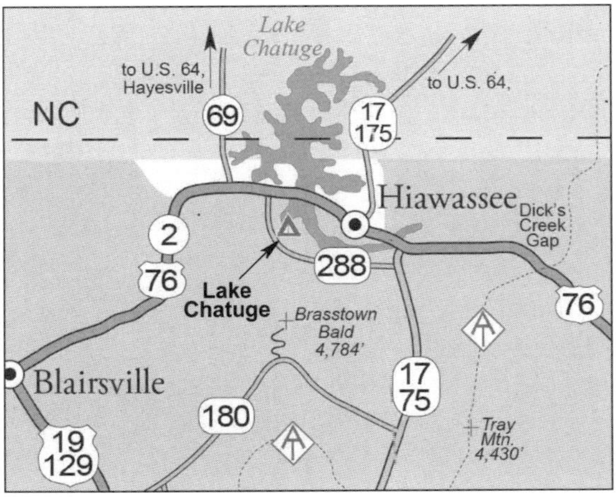

Lake Blue Ridge Recreation Area #78

Former USFS campground converted to day-use facility

Blue Ridge Ranger District
Chattahoochee National Forest
706.745.6928
GPS coordinates:
34.84819°N / 84.29029°W

- **loop trail**
- **fishing**
- **boating**
- **boat ramp**
- **campground closed**

Lake Blue Ridge is a favorite of sports fishermen. In fact, it is generally considered the only lake in Georgia where the feisty Muskie, a member of the Pike family, is found. It also features bass, bream, catfish, perch and crappie. With 3,290-acres of sparkling water pleasure boaters have a lot to get excited about as well. Lake Blue Ridge was formed in 1930 when the Blue Ridge dam was completed on the Toccoa River. Constructed by the Toccoa Electric Power Company it was the largest earthen dam in the Southeast at the time. The TVA purchased the facility in 1939.

The Lake Blue Ridge Recreation area is located on the western side of the lake. The forest service closed the campground here recently but visitors can still use the grounds. A short 0.6-mile loop runs through the old camping area and visitors can still fish from the banks, walk on the loop road and use the boat ramp.

Directions: Take U.S. 76 west from downtown Hiawassee for 2 miles. Turn left onto GA 288 and proceed one mile to the recreation area on the left.

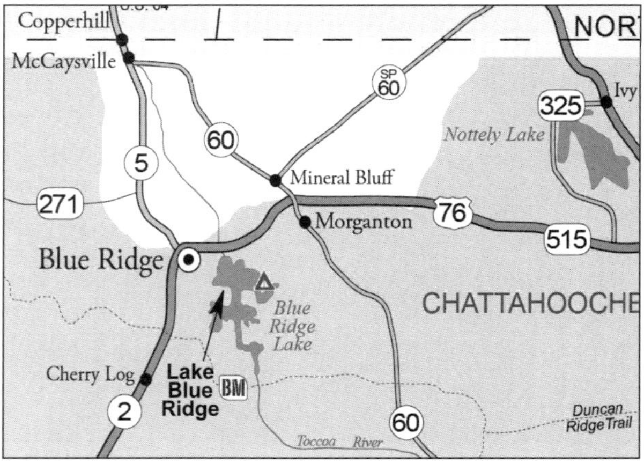

#79 Morganton Point Campground

Ideal for Lake Blue Ridge boaters and campers

Fishermen ply the calm waters of Lake Blue Ridge offshore of the picnic area

Blue Ridge Ranger District
Chattahoochee National Forest
706.745.6928
GPS coordinates:
34.869225°N / 84.24942°W

- **camping**
- **boat ramp**
- **fishing & boating**
- **picnicking**
- **seasonal**
- **user fee required**

Beautiful Lake Blue Ridge once had 2 scenic U.S. Forest Service campgrounds adorning its shores, but budget cuts and a slowing economy have taken their toll. With the closing of Lake Blue Ridge campground, Morganton Point Recreation Area now shoulders the Lake Blue Ridge camping load. Situated on the eastern shore of this 3,290-acre lake, Morganton Point offers 37 camping sites. Picnicking is great here as well with 13 tables and one covered picnic shelter. The campground also features a paved boat ramp for the scores of anglers and pleasure boaters who ply the sparkling waters of this massive TVA impoundment. Campers who visit the area in the summer can also take advantage of a large swimming beach and bath house.

Directions: From Blue Ridge take U.S. 515 north for 4 miles Turn right onto GA 60 and proceed into Morganton. There are several tricky turns and obscured road signs so just follow the brown U.S. Forest Service signs that direct you to the recreation area.

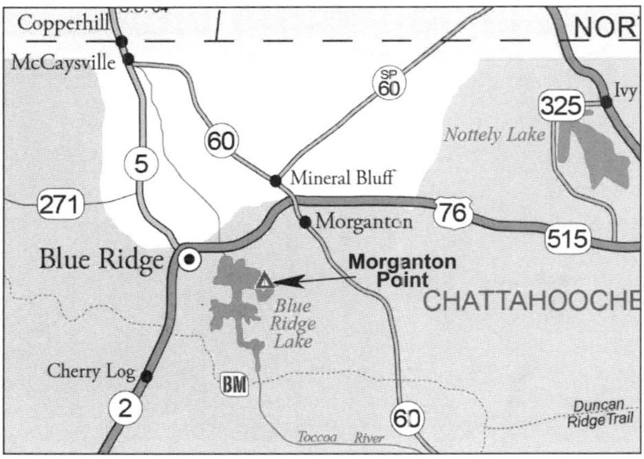

Lake Conasauga Recreation Area #80

Georgia's highest mountain lake

Conasauga Ranger District
Chattahoochee National Forest
706.695.6736
GPS coordinates:
34.8604°N / 84.6494°W

- **camping**
- **fishing**
- **boating with restrictions**
- **picnicking**
- **seasonal**
- **user fee required**

Nineteen-acre Lake Conasauga is one of the crown jewels of the spectacular North Georgia Mountains. Situated at a lofty 3,150' above sea level, Lake Conasauga is officially Georgia's highest mountain lake. It's cold, clear waters attract throngs of visitors on warm weather weekends and throughout the hot summer months. The name Conasauga comes from a Cherokee word *kahnasaga* which can mean "sparkling water," "grass," or "strong horse." Take your pick. The lake, recreation area and the bulk of the forest service roads throughout the Cohuttas were built by the Civilian Conservation Corps (CCC) during the depression years of the 1930s. This is a wild and wonderful area.

The campground has 34 campsites most ideally suitable for tents. Restroom facilities and water are centrally located in the campground. None of the camping sites are located directly on the lake but they are all close by.

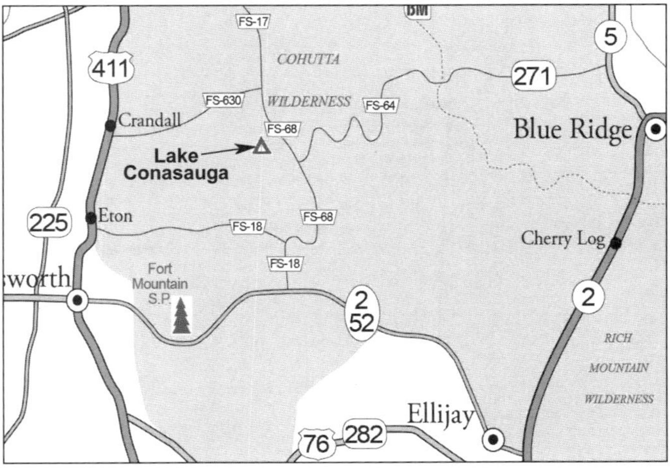

The day-use area features restrooms, picnic tables, grills, and two covered picnic shelters. The parking area is a short walk away but nothing too serious.

The recreation area also offers a swimming area, but not exactly what you would call a beach - more like a grassy ledge with a small boat dock. The lake is surprisingly cold even in the middle of the summer. Georgia's highest mountain lake, remember?

Anglers with small boats and pleasure boaters can enjoy the lake as well. The lake is limited to those powered by human horsepower or by electric motors only. A boat ramp will get you in the water with no worries.

Hiking Trails: Visitors come for the lake, but there's some pretty good hiking at Lake Conasauga as well. For starters, novices will like the 1.2-mile **Lake Conasauga Trail** that loops completely around the lake.

Wildlife lovers will enjoy the 1.7-mile **Songbird Trail** which begins at the lake outlet. Highlights include a beaver swamp and clear cuts within the Songbird Management Area which attract a wide variety of our fine feathered friends.

The 1.6-mile (one way) **Grassy Mountain Trail** climbs to an old tower atop Grassy Mountain. The summit offers spectacular views of the surrounding Cohutta mountains. The trail begins at the dam.

Directions:

From Chatsworth: Proceed north on U.S. 411 for 4 miles. Turn right at the traffic light in Eton and drive until the pavement ends. Continue ahead on what is now FS 18. Turn left onto FS 68 and proceed approximately 4 miles to the Barnes Creek picnic area. Continue an additional 6 miles to Lake Conasauga.

From Ellijay: Take GA 52 west for approximately 7 miles to FS 18 (look for the Lake Conasauga Recreation Area sign). Proceed along this road until the pavement ends to the junction with FS-68. Turn right and follow the signs to Lake Conasauga Recreation Area.

Barnes Creek Picnic Area #81

Roadside picnic area with a pretty cascading waterfall

Conasauga Ranger District
Chattahoochee National Forest
706.695.6736
GPS coordinates:
34.82570°N / 84.582513°W

- **small picnic area**
- **pretty cascade on Barnes Creek**

Exploring the Cohutta Wilderness by automobile is an adventure unto itself. Destinations like Jacks River Falls and Lake Conasauga require 15 or more miles of travel along rough Forest Service roads just to reach the trail heads. Occasionally a roadside destination beckons the traveller to stop and pause, even if only for just a moment. Such is the case with tiny Barnes Creek Picnic area which is located on the long road to Lake Conasauga. This very small picnic area is situated at 2,460' elevation and only has a few scant tables. It's claim to fame is a rocky 15' cascade along Barnes Creek that is alone worth a look. A footpath leads up a series of steps to an overlook at the top of the falls.

Directions: *From Chatsworth:* Proceed north on U.S. 411 for 4 miles. Turn right at the traffic light in Eton and drive until the pavement ends. Continue ahead on what is now FS 18. Turn left onto FS 68 and proceed approximately 4 miles to the Barnes Creek picnic area. Continue an additional 6 miles to Lake Conasauga.

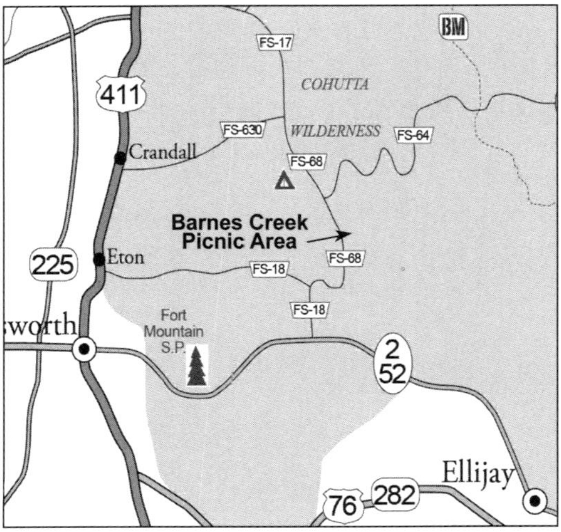

Note: The USFS roads in the Cohuttas can be confusing, and the best route to Lake Conasauga and Barnes Creek really depends on where you are coming from. It would be worth your while to invest a few bucks in a good road map to the area.

#82 The Pocket Recreation Area

Scenic secluded campground and day use area

Conasauga Ranger District
Chattahoochee National Forest
706.695.6736
GPS coordinates:
34.5855°N / 85.0834°W

- **campground**
- **picnic area**
- **hiking trail**

If you've never visited this isolated recreation area hemmed in on 3 sides by scenic Horn Mountain you really need to pay a visit. It's a surprisingly beautiful area of northwest Georgia. In the hot summer months the beautiful hardwood forest of oak, maple, hickory and poplar provide deep shade; in the fall the colors are spectacular.

Created by the Civilian Conservation Corps in 1938 for use as a camp, the foundations of several old CCC structures remain. The campground features 27 sites, most along the cold, clear spring fed creek, and day visitors have 17 picnic tables and one picnic shelter to enjoy. When you're done picnicking or playing in the magnificent creek you can stretch your legs on the 0.5-mile **Pocket Nature Trail**. If you're really looking to burn a few calories give the easy-to-moderate 2.5-mile **Pocket Loop Trail** a try.

Directions: From I-75 in Calhoun exit and take GA 136 approximately 14 miles northwest toward Villanow. About a half-mile east of Villanow turn left onto Pocket Road (County Road 230) and drive south for 7 miles to The Pocket on the left.

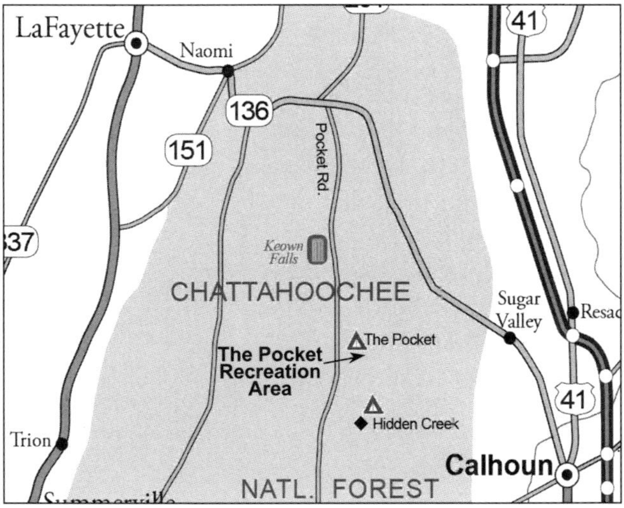

Hidden Creek Campground #83

Quiet, secluded campground near Calhoun

Conasauga Ranger District
Chattahoochee National Forest
706.695.6736
GPS coordinates:
34.82570°N / 84.582513°W

- **secluded tent camping**
- **no hiking trails**
- **no fees to camp**

Like The Pocket just a short drive to the north, secluded Hidden Creek campground is quite secluded. No, I mean *really* secluded. Hidden Creek is tucked into a cove between Calbeck Mountain on the western side and Horn Mountain to the east. One website describes it as being in the middle of nowhere (an assessment that I believe is pretty much spot-on).

The name Hidden Creek comes from the fact that the namesake stream seems to flow normally, then suddenly go dry. The 16-site tent campground is situated in a dense hardwood forest filled with beautiful oaks, maples and dogwoods. Unlike most other recreation areas in North Georgia there are no hiking trails but because it is so secluded visitors wishing to stretch their legs should be fine walking on FS 955. The campground has traditionally not required any type of fee, yet is rarely full. If you're looking for a secluded no-frills tent campground that provides a good base of operation in this part of the Chattahoochee National Forest, this may be your spot. Do be sure to tell someone where you are going.

Directions: From Calhoun take GA 156 south for 7.5 miles. Turn right onto Everett Springs Road and proceed 2 miles. Turn right onto Rock Creek Road and drive 3 miles. Turn right onto FS 955 and follow the signs to the recreation area.

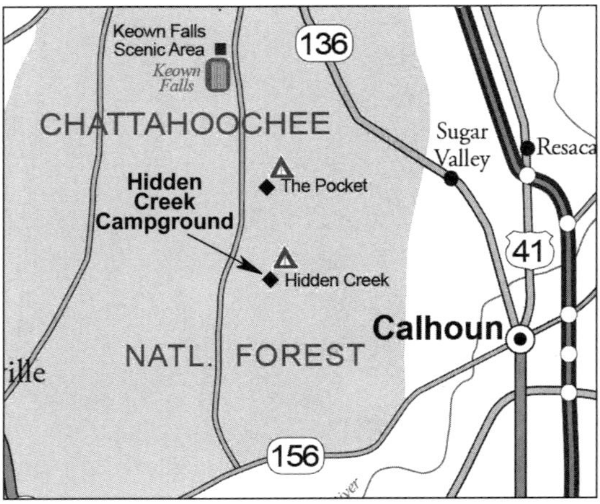

6

Just For The Fun Of It

Hit the Rivers #84, #85, #86, #87, #88

Opportunities for tubing, rafting, canoeing and kayaking

- **Chattahoochee River**
- **Chestatee River**
- **Etowah River**
- **Toccoa River**
- **Chattooga River**

Bull Sluice - Chattooga River

In the middle of a hot, sweltering Georgia summer even the normally cool mountains can get a bit steamy. What to do? Not to worry though as nature has its own perfect remedy for cooling off - hit the river! North Georgia features dozens of great streams to wade and fish and a surprisingly large number suitable for floating, whether it be tubing, rafting, canoeing or kayaking. I've listed five North Georgia rivers that offer great fun even for beginners. Here area a few you might take a look at:

Chattahoochee River #84

If you've ever been to Helen in the summertime you've no doubt witnessed the hundreds of tubers drifting peacefully down the playful Chattahoochee River. A number of vendors not only rent tubes but also run shuttles from Robertstown (just north of Helen) to a take-out on the south end of town. Check locally for the names of tubing vendors.

If whitewater action is your goal, then the nearly 20 miles of Class I-III whitewater beginning south of Helen may be just what you're looking for. The floating fun runs out when you hit the backwaters of Lake Lanier but the Chattahoochee River offers a great deal of fun as it spills out of the mountains. Here are a few suggestions if you canoe or kayak:

Upper Chattahoochee River

Section 2	Sautee Creek to GA 255 *calm with small shoals*	6 miles
Section 2	GA 255 to GA 115 *class I - II rapids*	5 miles
Section 3	GA 115 to Duncan Bridge *class I - III rapids*	4 miles

• *for more information on renting boats for the 'Hooch or to check into arranging a shuttle contact:*

Wildwood Outfitters
26 Megan Drive
Cleveland, GA 30528
1.800.553.2715

Chestatee River #85

Like the Chattahoochee, the Chestatee is a major Lake Lanier tributary river that winds through the Appalachian foothills. Located just east of Dahlonega the Chestatee offers over 20 miles of easy Class I - II whitewater interspersed with long, placid pools. This portion of the river is suitable for canoes, kayaks or tubes. More experienced boaters can start at Long Branch Road bridge which features the Class III Copper Mine rapid.

Beginners and those wanting to tube can run the 6-mile stretch from alongside GA 60 south of Dahlonega down to the GA 400 bridge. This section features playful Class I rapids and plenty of good scenery and is ideal for boaters with children.

Chestatee River

Section 2	Copper Mine to Lake Lanier *Class I - III rapids, great scenery*	18 miles
Section 2*	GA 60 to GA 400 bridge *Easy Class I with small shoals*	6 miles

* This middle portion of Section 2 is the most popular float for beginners or those with small children.

• *for more information on renting tubes or boats for the Chestatee River:*

Appalachian Outfitters
2084 South Chestatee / GA 60
Dahlonega, GA 30533
(located on GA 60, 3.5 miles from GA 400, 1/2 mile past the bridge)
GPS Coordinates: 34.50778N 83.973611W

Call the Appalachian Outfitters Chestatee River Outpost at 706.864.7117 for details and reservations.

Etowah River #86

Canoeing below Etowah Falls

Yet another great river for beginners and intermediate paddlers is the Etowah River, a major Lake Allatoona tributary. The most popular portion for paddlers is located just a few miles west and south of Dahlonega. The Etowah offers over 15 miles of easy Class I - III whitewater and plenty of splendid scenery. Of particular note is Etowah Falls, a 10' drop which can be portaged.

Section II features mostly flat water with a few small shoals but boasts one of the most unique features on any river, anywhere - an old tunnel nearly a quarter-mile long once used to divert the river so that the dry stream bed could be mined for gold. If the light at the far end is clearly visible and paddlers ascertain that the route is clear it is an unforgettable experience. A more detailed description of the river can be obtained on the web at: *www.americanwhitewater.org/content/River/detail/id/483*.

Etowah River

Section 2	GA 9 to Castleberry Bridge	6 miles
	Class I - III rapids, Etowah Falls	
Section 3	Castleberry Bridge to GA 136	8.8 miles
	Class I - II, Etowah tunnel	

• *for more information on booking Etowah River trips contact*:

inside the tunnel

Appalachian Outfitters
2084 South Chestatee / GA 60
Dahlonega, GA 30533
located on GA 60, 3.5 miles from GA 400
GPS Coordinates: 34.50778N 83.973611W

Call the Appalachian Outfitters
Chestatee River Outpost at
706.864.7117 for details and reservations

Toccoa River #87

This beautiful stream flows northwest from the Suches area into beautiful Lake Blue Ridge. At least one canoeing guidebook refers to the Toccoa River as the "prettiest whitewater stream in North Georgia" - high praise indeed! Beginning at Deep Hole Recreation Area the U.S. Forest Service has developed a 13.8-mile "canoe trail" that is suitable for novice paddlers and even tubers. This portion of the river features numerous Class I and II rapids and of course, magnificent river scenery. A number of trip options are possible and access is quite good throughout this entire section.

Toccoa River

Section 1	Deep Hole to Rock Creek Rd Bridge *Class I - II, good fishing section*	1.5 miles
Section 2	Rock Creek Road bridge to Margret	1 mile
Section 3	Margret to Butt bridge *Class I - II rapids, Benton MacKaye suspension bridge, campsites*	5.8 miles
Section 4	Butt bridge to Dial bridge	1.5 miles
Section 5	Dial bridge to Sandy Bottoms	5 miles

• *for more information on booking a Toccoa River trip contact:*

Jon Ron Toccoa River Outfitters
Blue Ridge, GA • 866.857.8758

Toccoa Valley Campground • 11481 Aska Road
Blue Ridge, GA 30513 • 706.838.4317

to float the river below Lake Blue Ridge:
Toccoa River Adventures • 340 Toccoa Ave.
McCaysville, Georgia 30555
706.492.5280

Chattooga River #88

Second Ledge (Class III) along the Chattooga's Section 3

One of the crown jewels of Southern Appalachian whitewater is the incomparable Chattooga Wild and Scenic River. Any person that loves rafting, canoeing or kayaking should float this magnificent river at least once in their lifetime. The Chattooga possesses an unmatched combination of scenic beauty and thundering whitewater. Better yet, the river progressively becomes more challenging as it flows south toward Lake Tugaloo providing clearly defined sections suitable for boaters of all skill levels.

The Chattooga gained notoriety in the early 1970s when the blockbuster *Deliverance* was filmed there. Just a few years later in 1974 the river was designated as a component of the National Wild and Scenic River system. The U.S. Forest Service carefully regulates the number of boaters that float the river and boaters must abide by a system of permits and regulations. If you're not an experienced boater but would still like to discover the mysteries of the Chattooga River, a number of highly experienced outfitters are available.

Chattooga Wild and Scenic River

Section 1	West Fork - Overflow Road to Longbottom Ford take out *Class I - II, good fishing section* *tubing is allowed*	4 miles
Section 2	Longbottom Ford to Earl's Ford *Class I - II, one Class III*	7 miles
Section 3	Earl's Ford to U.S. 76 *Class III - IV, one Class V* *intermediates to advanced only*	13 miles
Section 4	U.S. 76 to Lake Tugaloo *Class III - V, advanced only*	7 miles

• *for more information on booking a Chattooga River trip contact:*

Chattooga Whitewater Outfitters
14239 Hwy 76 (Long Creek Hwy)
Long Creek, SC 29658
Phone: 864.647.9083
www.cwo-hp.com

Nantahala Outdoor Center
Chattooga River Outpost
851 Chattooga Ridge Road
Mountain Rest, SC 29664
Phone: 864.647.9014 • Reservations: 888.905.7238
www.noc.com/whitewater-rafting/chattooga-river

Southeastern Expeditions • Chattooga River Outpost
7350 Hwy 76 E. • Clayton, GA 30525
Phone: 706.782.4331 • Reservations: 1.800.868.7238
www.southeasternexpeditions.com/Chattooga

Wildwater Ltd.
1251 Academy Road
Long Creek, SC 29658
Phone: 864.451.9972 • Reservations: 800.451.9972
www.wildwaterrafting.com/chattooga.php

Thar's Gold in them thar hills! #89

Strike it rich at the site of America's first great gold rush

- **Fun family activity**
- **Ideal "bad weather day" activity**
- **Historically significant**
- **Better odds than the lottery!**

Over 180 years after the discovery of gold near Dahlonega in 1828, people still come to the region to pan for the mystical, magical metal. With the price of gold soaring to historic levels nearly every week, the lure of gold will only increase with time. Gold was such a big business in North Georgia that in 1838 the U.S. Congress established the Dahlonega Mint as a branch of the U.S. Mint. The mint produced over $6 million worth of coins in its day (which translates into several hundred million in today's economy). As yields diminished and as a new gold rush commenced in California in 1849, "gold fever" subsided in North Georgia.

Even today a number of mines and panning sites are open to the public for gold and gemstone mining. The largest of these is Consolidated Gold Mines of Dahlonega which is also on the National Register of Historic Sites. Consolidated offers a fascinating underground mine tour as well as gold panning. The site was reportedly the largest gold mining operation east of the Mississippi in the late 1800s.

Most of the local mining establishments offer instructions on the classic panning method and several feature historic mining equipment exhibits and gem related gift shops. Additionally some offer gold panning contests and seasonal festivals. Dahlonega even holds its annual *Gold Rush Days* festival each October to honor its golden history.

Crisson Gold Mine
2736 Morrison Moore Pky East
Dahlonega, GA 30533
706.864.6363
www.crissongoldmine.com

Consolidated Gold Mine
185 Consolidated Gold Mine Rd
Dahlonega, GA 30533
706.864.8473
www.consolidatedgoldmine.com

Dukes Creek Mines
6145 Helen Highway
Sautee Nacoochee, GA 30571
706.878.2625
www.dukescreek.com

Gold 'n Gem Grubbin'
75 Gold Nugget Lane
Cleveland, GA 30528
706.865.5454
www.goldngem.com

#90 Riding the Mountain Rails

Follows the Toccoa River from Blue Ridge to McCaysville

Blue Ridge Scenic Railway
241 Depot Street
Blue Ridge, GA 30513
706.632.8724
800.934.1898
www.brscenic.com
GPS coordinates:
34.8686°N / 84.322°W

At the depot in downtown Blue Ridge

- **great sightseeing**
- **perfect family activity**
- **enjoyable shopping and dining opportunities**

Without a doubt one of the greatest ways to enjoy the magnificent scenery of North Georgia is by riding the rails. The wonderful Blue Ridge Scenic Railway has been in operation for a relatively short time (since 1998) but it has already become a prime North Georgia tourist destination. The line has deep historic roots in North Georgia dating back into the late 1800s when it was part of the Marietta & North Georgia Railroad, the Atlanta, Knoxville & Northern, and the Louisville & Nashville. The line operated under the Seaboard System and CSX into the 1980s as a freight carrier but eventually was abandoned and the railbed fell into disrepair. In 1990 a group of local investors bought the line and began the long and expensive process of restoring it as a scenic railway.

Today the railroad offers a scenic 26-mile round trip from downtown Blue Ridge along the beautiful Toccoa River to quaint McCaysville on the Georgia/Tennessee line. Actually McCaysville sort of "shares" a town with Copperhill, Tennessee. These 2 towns are differentiated only by the state line that divides them. The BRSR stops here and tourists can disembark for an hour or two of shopping, sightseeing or dining.

Upon your return to beautiful downtown Blue Ridge be sure to take some time and explore this quaint village. With the establishment of the railroad the old downtown section along the railroad tracks and depot have gone through a wonderful revitalization. Dozens of interesting shops and delightful eateries line the streets. Be sure to call ahead and check the railroad's schedule and make reservations well in advance if you're coming during a peak time. Visit the railway's website as well to find out about the special excursions offered throughout the year.

BabyLand General® #91

Home of the world-famous Cabbage Patch Kids®

BabyLand General Hospital
300 N.O.K. Drive
Cleveland, GA 30528
706.865.2171
www.cabbagepatchkids.com
GPS coordinates:
34.6166°N / 83.75°W

- **mandatory kids destination**
- **recently relocated and expanded location**

Whether you are a youngster or just young at heart one of the must-see destinations in northeast Georgia is the delightful BabyLand General® Hospital, home of the adorable and world-renowned Cabbage Patch Kids®. Visitors come from near and far to visit this most unique hospital and most wind up "adopting" one (or more) of these cuddly kids, some right from birth. If you've never witnessed the delivery process you're in for a real treat.

Once you've taken the "Oath of Adoption" it's official - you have a new addition to the family. If you're like most people who visit you'll have a hard time stopping at just one of these adorable Cabbage Patch Kids®, the creations of Xavier Roberts. Many a child (and grown-up) has fallen under the spell of these little people and some have adopted an entire family. In all seriousness Cabbage Patch Kids® are extremely collectible with some of the early "kids" reportedly worth in the tens of thousands of dollars.

A few years back the hospital moved from off the Cleveland square to a wonderful 100-acre property just north of town that looks like a magnificent Southern plantation house. The expanded gift shop has every accessory needed to complete the adoption process and keep your little addition dressed well. The medical staff on hand is certainly correct when they say, "this is like no hospital you've ever visited!"

Directions: From the square in downtown Cleveland take U.S. 129 north for 0.3 mile. Turn right onto GA 75 toward Helen and proceed 1.5 miles. Turn left onto Hulsey Road and proceed 0.5 mile. Turn right onto N.O.K. Drive. Follow N.O.K. Drive until you see the graceful white columns of BabyLand General® Hospital.

#92 In Search of the Elusive Trout

Hundreds of miles of spectacular streams and rivers

- **brook, brown and rainbow trout**
- **seasonal and year round streams**
- **catch your limit or catch-and-release**

Chattooga River at Burrells Ford

There is plenty of great fishing in North Georgia, but for many anglers there's nothing quite like the challenge of catching a native trout. The North Georgia region features hundreds of miles of great trout waters containing both native brook and rainbow trout as well as stocked brook, brown and rainbow trout. Contrary to popular opinion, you don't have to be a sophisticated fly fisherman possessing thousands in fancy equipment to enjoy trout fishing. Here on North Georgia's beautiful streams, mountain natives join the well-equipped tourist to enjoy this great angling passion.

There are a number of books and maps that detail North Georgia's popular trout waters and you would be well-served to take a look before deciding on a destination. Also be sure to familiarize yourself with the rules and regulations; the penalties for not doing so can be severe.

The Chattahoochee National Fish Hatchery and the Lake Burton Fish Hatchery produce hundreds of thousands of trout for the rivers and streams of North Georgia so there are plenty of fish to go around. Listed below are just a few popular trout fishing destinations for novices. A number of excellent outfitters and guide services are also available to teach you proper trout fishing techniques as well as get you stocked up on all the latest equipment and flies. You can get all the help you need to become an expert trout angler and hopefully you'll "land the big one" next time out. Here are a few streams to consider:

Jacks River - Cohutta Wilderness (north central)
Conasauga River - Cohutta Wilderness (north central)
Toccoa River (below the dam) - (north central)
Cooper Creek - (north central)
Chattooga River - (northeast corner)
Dick's Creek - (northeast)
Chattahoochee River - (northeast)
Dukes Creek - (northeast)
Upper Tallulah River - (northeast)

Here are a few North Georgia fishing outfitters you may wish to contact:

Unicoi Outfitters
7280 South Main Street • Helen, GA 30545
www.unicoioutfitters.com • 706.878.3083
also located at -
490 E. Main Street • Blue Ridge, GA 30513
706.632.1880

Reel'em In Guide Service
1890 Burnt Mountain Road • Ellijay, Georgia 30536
706.635.5472 local home • 706.273.0764 cell
www.reeleminguideservice.com

Cohutta Fishing company
487 East Main Street • Cartersville, GA 30121
770.606.1100 • www.cohuttaafishingco.com

North Georgia Outfitters
83 West 1st Street • Dawsonville, GA 30534
678.414.9317 • 678.410.7529
www.northgeorgiaoutfitters.com

Tritt's Outfitters
550 Grove Street North • Dahlonega, GA 30533
(706) 864-1732 • www.flyfishnga.com

Reel Job Fishing, LLC
3 Noontootla Overlook • Blue Ridge, GA 30513
770.330.7583 • www.kent-klewein.com

Dillard House Stables & Fly Fishing
768 Franklin Street, Dillard, GA 30537
706.746.2038 • www.dillardhousestables.com

The Buckhead House
(trout fishing equipment)
130 North Main Street • Hiawassee, GA 30546
706.896.0028

#93 Saddle Up

Hundreds of miles of spectacular streams and rivers

- **a number of local stables offer a variety of riding options**
- **guided rides or solo**
- **perfect activity for all ages**

There is nothing quite like experiencing the grandeur of the North Georgia mountains from atop one of nature's most noble beasts - the horse. Perhaps horseback riding causes us to identify with those early pioneers and settlers who depended on horsepower for transportation and much of the labor needed on the early farms across the region.

Today visitors can choose from an ample number of reputable stables scattered across North Georgia that give you the opportunity to get off your feet and into the saddle. Here's a partial listing of stables that offer horseback riding in the beautiful North Georgia mountains:

Gold City Corral • 49 Forrest Hill S. Road
Dahlonega, GA 20533 • 706.867.9395 • www.goldcitycorral.com

Sunburst Stables • 3181 Hwy. 255 • Clarkesville, GA 30523
706.947.RIDE • 800.806.1953 • www.sunburststables.com

Trackrock Stables • 202 Trackrock Camp Road
Blairsville, GA 30512 • 706.745.5252

Dillard House Stables & Fly Fishing • 768 Franklin Street
Dillard, GA 30537 • 706.746.2038 • www.dillardhousestables.com

---

Fort Mountain Stables • 548 Cliff Mine Roads
Chatsworth, GA 30705 • 706.517.4906 • www.fortmountainstables.net

---

Blanche Manor Horseback Riding • 177 Deal Hollow Road
Copperhill, TN 37317 • 706.455.7433 • www.blanchemanor.com

Flying Through the Forest #94

Zip lining is a thrilling new way to see the mountains

- **exciting variety of high altitude adventures**
- **excellent supervision and preparation**

There's a new way to experience the mountains, and it's not for the faint of heart. It's called zip lining, and if you haven't tried it you're literally in for the ride of your life. If you think you know all about it, think again; it's quite a bit more than a simple slide down a suspended line. Some of the current operators feature multi-hour "adventures" with multiple zip lines through the forest and over ponds as well as ropes and sky bridge adventures. It's sort of akin to whitewater boating in the treetops. Here are just a few companies that offer zip line adventures in the area.

North Georgia Canopy Tours
5290 Harris Road, Lula, GA 30554
770.869.7272 • www.northgeorgiacanopytours.com

Chattooga Ridge Canopy Tours
Wildwater Chattooga Ridge Adventure Center
1251 Academy Road, Long Creek, SC 29658
866.319.8870 • www.wildwaterrafting.com/chazip.php

Sunburst Stables
3181 Hwy. 255 • Clarkesville, GA 30523
706.947.RIDE • 800.806.1953 • www.sunburststables.com

Fire Wire Zip Lines
1408 Appalachian Hwy. • Blue Ridge, GA 30513
706.946.1010 • www.firewireziplines.com

Lake Lanier Canopy Tours
7000 Holiday Road • Buford, GA 30518
770.828.7654 • www.lakelaniercanopytours.com

ZipNTime
7019 S. Main St. • Helen, GA 30545
706.878.ZIPS (9477) • www.zipntime.com

#95 Two-wheeled Adventures

North Georgia offers an ever growing selection of biking options

- **over 70 mountain bike trails across North Georgia**
- **hundreds of miles of backcountry roads and challenging scenic roads**

Whether you're a mountain biker or a road warrior, North Georgia is great when experienced on two wheels. The U.S. Forest Service and the state parks have started to recognize that more and more visitors want to see the sights atop their personal bicycle and new trails are being developed all the time. In fact, one internet site claims that there are now over 70 mountain biking trails in North Georgia.

There are a number of good resources in print to help you identify roads suitable for riding, so have at it. Here is a listing of a few North Georgia bike shops sure to have the equipment or information you need to get rolling. Spend a half hour on Google and you'll come up with dozens of great biking options. Here are a few local shops to help out as well:

Cartecay River Bicycle Shop
3 miles east of Ellijay on GA 52 • Ellijay, GA 30540
706.635.BIKE • www.cartecaybikes.com

Cycle South • 544 East Main Street Suite 3 • Blue Ridge, GA 30513-4240 • 706.632.3533 • www.cyclesouth.net

---

Blairsville Bikes and Boards • 357 Murphy Hwy. Ste. 2
Blairsville, GA 30512 • 706-745-8141

Bike Town USA • 1604 Dawsonville Hwy.
Gainesville, GA 30501 • 770-532-7090 • www.biketownusa.com

Adventure Cycles
7429 Spout Springs Road • Flowery Branch, GA 30542
770-695-0204 • www.adventurecycles.com

Habersham Bicycles • 152 Anderson Circle • Alto, GA 30510
706-894-2453 • www.habershambicycles.com

One-of-a-kind Shoppes #96

Reflecting the heritage and culture of the region

Every town has at least one store or shop that is an experience unto itself. To compile a list and call it comprehensive would be pointless, but here are a few places to visit that you might call...*unique*. There are scores more - let us know who you think needs to be included.

The Old Sautee Store

Dahlonega General Store - On the square in Dahlonega, this old general store features collectibles, cookbooks, peanuts & jams, old-fashioned candy and lots, lots more. **www.dahlonegageneralstore.com**

Goats on the Roof - Besides goats on the roof (really) this fascinating establishment features gold panning, jams, jellies, ice cream and souvenirs. Located on U.S. 441 south of Clayton. **www.goats-on-the-roof.com**

Tallulah Point Overlook - Located directly on the rim of rugged Tallulah Gorge on the scenic loop, TPO offers the only roadside overlook of the gorge. Great collection of books, souvenirs, refreshments and more. **www.tallulahpoint.com**

Foxfire Museum Gift Shop - Offers a wide range of regional folk pottery, hand-woven textiles, home-made soaps, and a huge selection of books about Southern Appalachia, including the Foxfire series. **www.foxfire.org**

Mark of the Potter - Located in historic Watts Mill on the beautiful Soquee River. Features all types of unique pottery from over 40 artists. 9982 Hwy 197, 2 miles south of Batesville. **www.markofthepotter.com**

Mountain Crossings at Walasi-yi - Situated right smack in the middle of the Appalachian Trail at Neels Gap on U.S. 129. Top-of-the-line hiking and backpacking gear, books, crafts, gifts and refreshments. Located halfway between Blairsville and Cleveland. **www.mountaincrossings.com**

Mercier Orchards - Whether you want to pick their famous apples or just eat them this is a great place to visit at any time. Country store and orchards. 8660 Blue Ridge Dr. (Hwy 5) Ellijay. **www.mercier-orchards.com**

Nora Mill Granary - Located on the banks of the Chattahoochee River just south of Helen, this historic 130+ year old mill is still in operation. Grits, jellies bread mix and more. **www.noramill.com**

Burt's Farm - Just down the road from Amicalola Falls State Park, Burt's is a must-see in the fall when it becomes a sea of orange. Hayrides, gifts, eats, etc. 5 Burt's Farm Road, Dawsonville. **www.burtsfarm.com**

#97 Step Up to the Plate

World-famous cuisine is at the top of the list

North Georgia offers some great dining experiences, but not everyone agrees on what constitutes good dining. There are hundreds of awesome places to eat, but these are a few places (great food/unique atmosphere) that are my favorites when it comes time to chow down. If you operate an establishment that's not on this list, don't be mad - invite me to dinner! Check with the local chamber for more ideas.

The Dillard House *(southern home cooking)*
768 Franklin Street, Dillard • 706.746.5348 • www.dillardhouse.com

The Cupboard Cafe *(American fare)*
7388 Hwy. 441 • Dillard • 706.746.5700 • www.thecupboardcafe.com

Oinkers *(barbeque)*
2353 Hwy. 441 S. • Clayton • 706.754.7010

Manrique's *(Mexican)*
611 Hwy. 441 S. • Clayton • 706.782.5815

Glen Ella Springs *(fine dining)*
1789 Bear Gap Road • Clarkesville • 706.754.7295 • www.glenella.com

The Attic *(casual dining)*
1344 Washington St. • Clarkesville • 706.839.1811 • www.theatticrestaurant.com

Nacoochee Village Tavern Pizzeria *(pizza and sandwiches)*
7275 S. Main St. • Helen • 706.878.0199 • www.villagetavernpizza.com

Michalee's Chocolate Caffe *(specializing in desserts!)*
142 N. Main St. • Hiawassee • 706.896.2752 • www.michaelees.com

The Oaks *(American fare, seafood, steaks)*
3499 Hwy. 76 W. • Hiawassee • 706.896.4141 • www.theridgesresort.com

Aviator Cafe *(American fare)*
342 Blue Ridge St. Suite H • Blairsville • 706.781.1043

The Smith House *(southern home cooking)*
84 S. Chestatee St. • Dahlonega • 706.867.7000 • www.smithhouse.com

The Pink Pig *(barbeque)*
824 Cherry Log St. • Cherrylog • 706.276.3311 • www.budspinkpig.com

Harvest on Main *(American fare)*
576 E. Main St. • Blue Ridge • 706.946.6164 • www.harvestonmain.com

Blue Ridge Brewery *(American fare)*
187 Depot St. • Blue Ridge • 706.632.6611 • www.w.blueridgebrewery.com

Cantaberry Restaurant *(American fare)*
51 River St. • Ellijay • 706.636.4663

Jolly Roger Seafood Market & Grill *(seafood)*
716 Industrial Blvd. • Ellijay • 706.276.2090

go to www.tripadvisor.com/Restaurants for customer reviews...

Festivals and Special Events #98

Reflecting the heritage and culture of the region

Some of the best fun and good times can be enjoyed without ever leaving Main Street. Gaze over this *very incomplete* listing of some of the larger and more well-known festivals. Visit the websites of your favorite town or county for a complete schedule of events.

April		
Gold Panning Championships	Dahlonega	3rd weekend April
A Taste of Toccoa	Toccoa	mid-April
Foxfire Living History Days	Mountain City	mid-April
Bear on the Square Music & Folk Fest.	Dahlonega	mid-April
Celebrate Clayton	Clayton	late April
May		
Rhododendron Festival	Hiawassee	beginning of May
Dawsonville Spring Fling Festival	Dawsonville	early May
Mountain Laurel Festival	Clarkesville	mid-May
Arts in the Park	Blue Ridge	late May
June		
Georgia Mtn. Roots & Music Festival	Hiawassee	early June
Helen to the Atlantic Hot Air Balloon Race	Helen	June
"The Reach of Song" historic drama	Young Harris	summer months
July		
Appalachian Wagon Train	Chatsworth	early July
Old Timers Day	Blue Ridge	Sat @ July 4
Mountain Fair	Hiawassee	late July
August		
Bluegrass and Barbeque Festival	Dillard	early August
September		
Labor Day Barbeque	Blue Ridge	Labor Day
Apple Pickin' Jubilee	Ellijay	Sept. - Oct.
Oktoberfest	Helen	mid-Sept - early Nov.
October		
Cherry Log Festival	Cherry Log	early October
Foxfire Mountaineer Festival	Clayton	1st weekend Oct.
Big Red Apple Festival	Cornelia	mid-October
Sorghum Festival	Blairsville	mid-October
Georgia Apple Festival	Ellijay	mid-October
Gold Rush Days	Dahlonega	3rd weekend Oct.
Mountain Moonshine Festival	Dawsonville	late October
November		
Light Up Blue Ridge	Blue Ridge	Sat. after Thanksg.
Babyland's Appalachian Christmas	Cleveland	late November

#99 Chambers of Commerce

FUN begins with the right information

It's just good common sense. When you're exploring a new area and you want the latest 411 on where to go to have fun, what to see and where to eat, a good place to start is at the local chamber or visitor center. Here are a few chamber locations to get you started on your next North Georgia trip:

Blairsville / Union County Chamber of Commerce
385 Welcome Center Lane • Blairsville, GA 30514
877.745.5789 • 706.745.5789 • www.blairsvillechamber.com

Chatsworth - Murray County Chamber of Commerce
126 North 3rd Avenue • Chatsworth, GA 30705
706.695.6060 • www.murraycountychamber.org

Dade County Chamber of Commerce
111 Railway Lane • Trenton, GA 30752
706.657.4488 • www.dadechamber.com

Dahlonega Convention and Visitors Bureau
101 South Park St. • Dahlonega 30533
706.864.3711 • 800.231.5543 • www.dahlonega.org

Fannin County Chamber of Commerce
152 Orvin Lance Drive • Blue Ridge, GA 30513
706.632.5680 • www.blueridgemountains.com

Gilmer County Chamber of Commerce
P.O. Box 505 • 368 Craig Street • Ellijay, GA 30540
706.635.7400 • www.gilmerchamber.com

Habersham County Chamber of Commerce
668 Clarkesville Street • Cornelia, GA 30531
706.864.3711 • 800.231.5543 • www.habershamchamber.com

Helen Welcome Center / White County Con. & Visitors Bureau
726 Brucken Strasse • Helen, GA 30545
706.778.4654 • www.helenga.org

Rabun County Welcome Center / Chamber of Commerce
P.O. Box 750 • 232 Hwy. 441 North • Clayton, GA 30525
706.782.4812 • www.gamountains.com

Towns County Chamber of Commerce
1411 Jack Dayton Circle • Young Harris, GA 30582
800.984.1543 • 706.896.4966 • www.mountaintopga.com

White County Chamber of Commerce
122 North Main Street • Cleveland, GA 30528
706.865.5356 • www.whitecountychamber.org

Chattahoochee National Forest

www.fs.usda.gov

Chattahoochee National Forest - District Offices

Blue Ridge District
2042 Highway 515 West
Blairsville, GA 30512
Phone: (706) 745-6928
Fax: 706 745-7494
Monday-Friday
8:00 a.m. - 4:30 p.m.

Conasauga District
3941 Highway 76
Chatsworth, GA 30705
Phone: (706) 695-6736
Fax: (706) 695-1872
Monday - Friday
8:00 a.m. - 4:30 p.m.

Chattooga District
9975 Highway 441 S
Lakemont, GA 30552
Phone: (706) 754-6221
Monday - Friday
8:00 a.m. - 4:30 p.m.

Chattahoochee-Oconee National Forest - Supervisor's Office
1755 Cleveland Highway
Gainesville, GA 30501
Phone: (770) 297-3000
Mon-Thur 8:00 a.m. - 4:30 p.m.

The Chattahoochee National Forest encompasses over 750,000 acres in 18 North Georgia counties. It includes over 2,200 miles of rivers and streams, over 450 miles of hiking and recreational trails, and 1,600 miles of roads. The name *Chattahoochee* is believed to originate from the native Cherokee and Creek Indians, meaning "river of the painted (or flowering) rock." It is the starting point for the famed Appalachain Trail and is the home of the Chattooga Wild and Scenic River and the Chattahoochee River. It also boasts 10 outstanding wilderness areas:

Big Frog Wilderness
8,082 acres along the GA-TN border (89 acres in Georgia)

Blood Mountain Wilderness
7,800 acres

Brasstown Wilderness
12,896 acres

Cohutta Wilderness
36,977 acres
(35,268 acres in Georgia)

Ellicott Rock Wilderness
8,274 acres
(2,021 acres in Georgia)

Mark Trail Wilderness
16,400 acres

Raven Cliffs Wilderness
9,115 acres

Rich Mountain Wilderness
9,476 acres

Southern Nantahala Wilderness
23,474 acres
(11,770 acres in Georgia)

Tray Mountain Wilderness
9,702 acres

North Georgia State Parks

www.gastateparks.org

Amicalola Falls State Park and Lodge • Dawsonville
56 rooms • picnic shelters • 14 cottages • 24 campsites
(706) 265-4703 • Lodge Reservations (800) 573-9656

Black Rock Mountain State Park • Mountain City
2 picnic shelters • 10 cottages • 14 cottages • 44 campsites
pioneer camp • (706) 746-2141 • Open 3/16-11/30

Cloudland Canyon State Park • Rising Fawn
5 picnic shelters • 1 group shelter • 16 cottages
72 campsites • 12 backcountry sites • 4 pioneer camps
(706) 657-4050

Fort Mountain State Park • Chatsworth
7 picnic shelters • 1 group shelter • 15 cottages
70 campsites • 4 backcountry sites • pioneer camp
(706) 422-1932

James H. (Sloppy) Floyd State Park • Summerville
5 picnic shelters • 1 group shelter • 16 cottages
72 campsites • 12 backcountry sites • 4 pioneer camps
(706) 857-0826

Moccasin Creek State Park • Clarkesville
1 picnic shelter • 55 campsites • (706) 947-3194
Open 3/16-11/30

Smithgall Woods State Park • Helen
3 picnic shelters • 5 cottages • 2 pioneer camps
(706) 878-3087

Tallulah Gorge State Park • Tallulah Falls
2 picnic shelters • 50 campsites • 3 backcountry sites
pioneer camp • (706) 754-7981 • camping (706) 754-7979

Unicoi State Park and Lodge • Helen
100 rooms • 6 picnic shelters • 1 group shelter • 30 cottages
82 campsites • (706) 878-2201 • lodge (800) 573-9659

Vogel State Park • Blairsville
4 picnic shelters • 1 group shelter • 35 cottages • 103 campsites
4 backcountry sites • pioneer camp • (706) 745-2628

INDEX

About the author - Brian A. Boyd

A lifelong hiker, avid outdoorsman and amateur photographer, Brian Boyd published his first southern Appalachian guidebook, *The Chattooga Wild and Scenic River,* back in 1990. That same year Brian founded Fern Creek Press as a small, independent publisher of local guidebooks and maps.

In the twenty years since, Boyd has published over fifteen guidebooks describing some of his favorite areas and detailing topics of local historical interest. Some of Boyd's other works include *Waterfalls of the Southern Appalachians* (five editions), *The Highlands-Cashiers Outdoors Companion, Boyd's Guide to Georgia's Rabun County, Yesterday's Rabun, Summits of the South, The Great Smoky Mountains Pocket Companion, The Tallulah Falls Railroad - A Photographic Remembrance*, and *Secrets of Tallulah*.

The mission of Fern Creek Press is to publish easy-to-use niche guides that explore the southern Appalachian region. Some of these books detail subjects that normally would not attract big-name publishers. Boyd's simple straight-forward narratives contain concise, accurate information in an easy-to-use format and at a reasonable price. What you may not know is that Boyd personally handles the entire project including writing, photography, maps, layout and the distribution of his publications as well. In his spare time he continues to explore the southern Appalachian region and write and publish new projects. Brian and his wife, Kay, currently live in Clarkesville. They have three grown children.

Boyd enjoys speaking to church or civic groups about his passion for the natural wonders and history of the region. He can be reached at 706.982.3635.

John 3:16 • Proverbs 3:5-6

Notes